For

Ma___ ___ ind __ __ ever

with the hop___ __
enjoy __ book a __
__ the __

Ev___ Reave H___

ONE SAINT AND
SEVEN SINNERS

ENNEN REAVES HALL

One
SAINT
and
SEVEN
SINNERS

Thomas Y. Crowell Company

New York · Established 1834

*The Library of Congress has catalogued
this publication as follows:*

Hall, Ennen Reaves. One saint and seven sinners. New York,
  Crowell [1959] 243 p. 21 cm. 1. Clergymen's families. I.
  Title. BV4396.H3 253.2 58–14308 ‡

To all the pioneer missionaries
who sowed the seed
for today's fruitful church
this book is dedicated

This book is not fiction, but a faithful recording of life as lived by a missionary's family in the early years of this century. Primarily it is a portrait of my parents, but it has a deeper significance; for it is also a documentary picture of a way of life that has little in common with this highly mechanized and scientific age; and of an approach to life and religion even less like that of the present day.

It was the Christ, whose disciple my father and his contemporaries were, who said: "Except a corn of wheat fall into the ground and die, it abideth alone; but if it die, it bringeth forth much fruit." Whatever mistakes were theirs in theory or practice, the fruit of the labors of these early-day ministers attests to their death in Christ Jesus.

ENNEN REAVES HALL

ONE SAINT AND
SEVEN SINNERS

1

Papa was a big man, both physically and spiritually. Standing six feet four and having a booming voice that would need no amplifier even in one of today's vast auditoriums, he was a commanding figure when he stood up to speak. He had a heavy mustache and a shock of black hair that he kept on end by combing his hands through it.

Spiritually, all his church members and the town agreed, Papa was a saint. In fact, that status was as often attributed to him by the non-churchgoing element as by his loyal members.

And, with similar accord, all agreed that Papa headed a houseful of sinners, imported to the Indian Territory from Texas.

Papa, like John the Baptist, had been preaching his Christ in that wilderness which was known to us as the Indian Territory over a year before we joined him there in the first year of the new century. There were then six sinners, counting Mamma and Mamma had to be counted. No matter how much opinions might differ about Mamma, she was never ignored.

So short she could stand under Papa's outstretched arm, so slight a strong wind might have lifted her off the ground, she was always someone to reckon with. She had hair of

1

brick red, flashing deep blue eyes, a quick tongue, and a strong mind that could not be swayed by popular opinion. The combination often brought about situations that made people stand a little in awe of Mamma, put them instinctively on their guard when she was around. I'm sure she knew, but didn't really care, that she was placed in the same category as her brood of young sinners. It was this disdain of the judgment of others that set Mamma a little apart from the crowd.

We sinners recognized Mamma as one of us, in spite of the fact that she was the actual ruler of our household, severe in her dictums and trigger quick in her reprimands, which might, without warning, take the form of corporal assault—something Papa seldom resorted to. Yet it was Papa, rather than Mamma, whom we most feared.

For one thing, Papa expected to find his own saintly qualities in us, so that we knew we could expect little sympathy from him for our worldly leanings. But Mamma talked our language; she seemed to understand the power of our temptations. There was always a chance that we could wheedle Mamma into giving us our way, and we felt we could count on her to be a buffer against Papa's righteous indignation or even the open disapproval of the church members when our sins became community affairs. Mamma, we instinctively felt, shared in our rebellion against the solitary pedestal upon which the church thought the offspring of a saint like Papa should be placed.

For another thing, Papa's punishment was far more to be dreaded than any reaction from Mamma's quick temper. Papa prayed over us when we stood before him in judgment—prayed aloud and with anguish, while we squirmed and tried vainly to escape the lash of our own guilty consciences. To displease Papa, and be caught, was to be brought face to face with God. Who wouldn't prefer the stinging palm of Mamma's hand or the biting lash of the peach-tree switch? But as long as we could keep our sins hidden from Papa, our rebellious young hearts took it for granted that we had also put one over on God. Papa, in a sense, was God to us.

So much for the situation that inspires this saga. As for the background, it might be best to leave the Indian Territory town unnamed. Some who read this today might travel through that prosperous little city in Oklahoma and search in vain for signposts that have long since disappeared.

Suffice it to say that the thriving little incorporated community boasted a population of about fifteen hundred in 1900. Except for saloons, forbidden in the Indian Territory by the government, any Western movie set with its two-block-long, dusty Main Street would pass for our town. We had the false-front, one-story buildings, with the upper windows giving the illusion of a second story when viewed from the front; the rattling board sidewalks; the hitching rails. We also boasted of the only tax-supported public school in the Territory, a railroad station, a hotel with six rooms to rent, and three churches and a half. The half was the Episcopal Church building, long unused for lack of enough members to support even a part-time rector. Added to the civic improvements was a recently completed, commodious six-room parsonage that it had taken Papa a full year to build over the bitter protests of some of his members. Most of the money to pay for the material he had collected from among his Texas friends, and he had added many hours of his own labor to that donated by the men of the church.

The people, Papa always said feelingly, were good people. Doubtless they were no different from all the people in all the small towns of today, but they appeared so in some ways because the customs and the thinking of the times were different.

3

Having been at his missionary outpost a year ahead of us, Papa rather had the edge on us in popularity. An outbreak of black smallpox, occurring soon after he arrived to take up his duties as full-time pastor of the Baptist Church, had not only served to delay our coming but had won for Papa his canonization. During the weeks that the epidemic raged he had fearlessly nursed the sick, who often were deserted by their fearstricken neighbors, and buried the dead when others feared contamination, walking serenely through it all without appearing to suffer from fatigue or lack of sleep, and apparently immune to a disease so highly contagious that the very name of it brought terror into the hearts of other men.

After that, how could five troublesome youngsters be taken into the hearts of his idolatrous congregation? Or a small woman with a sharp tongue appear worthy to be his mate? We were equally disappointed in the town because we had expected it to be wildly exciting, with cowboys and Indians waging battles before our eyes, so no doubt the devil Papa preached about pounced gleefully upon the situation and made the most of it.

The church members who waited on the cinder island of the Santa Fe box station on that hot September day in 1900, along with their pastor, must have been disappointed by their first glimpse of what they had wished upon their town. Certainly they had no reason to feel reassured as we climbed off that train, for after the day-and-night journey in a sweltering day coach we presented a sorry spectacle indeed.

First there was Red. His hair was so fiery that older boys often pretended to warm their hands over it. Fifteen and gangling, he had a generous supply of freckles of the same bright hue. He still wore short pants for the sole reason that there was no money to buy long ones. Because he had stubbed his toe before leaving Texas and infection had set in, Red wore

4

one shoe in his hip pocket while from the other pocket protruded the handle of the small ax with which he kept Mamma supplied with kindling wood. Red believed in preparedness for battle.

Rusty, two years younger, also had won his name because of his hair. It was neither black nor brown nor red but a combination of all three, and so wavy that only the fact that Rusty was quick with his fists kept him from being tagged Curly. Until he became angry, he was a strikingly handsome boy. Then his eyes crossed ludicrously, a signal with which we were all familiar. Like Mamma, Rusty was an individualist and strictly a nonconformist. Because he hated wearing shoes, he'd taken his off, stuffed his stockings inside his blouse, and tied the strings of the shoes together and slung them about his neck, the holes in the soles staring at everyone like unblinking eyes. In addition he wore a slingshot across one shoulder, a bow and quiver of arrows across the other. Rusty, too, believed in preparedness.

Third in line, I had the uneasy place of middle child and was the only one who didn't rate a full-time nickname. When the boys wanted to tease me they called me Skinny-legs, not knowing that I secretly preferred that to my own odd name. The descriptive term must have fitted me, as Mamma said my legs seemed to sprout out of my chin and were the most noticeable things about my thin frame. My dark brown hair was extremely curly, and because I had kept my head out of the window most of the time en route from Texas, resulting in the loss of my hat, I probably resembled a species such as the Territory homesteaders had never seen.

Always trying to emulate my hero, Rusty, I had also taken off my patent-leather slippers, but Mamma hadn't noticed. Because they had no ties I could only button the straps of one to the other and wear them bracelet style across my arm.

In the pocket of my dress was Rusty's prized possession, a huge jackknife, which he'd thrust into my hand in a burst of generosity as our journey drew near its end. "Here, Skinny, you can have it," he'd fairly startled me by saying. "And don't you be scared to use it if an Injun takes after you."

Dutch, almost four years younger than I, was the family pet because she had been ill so much of her life. Nothing was ever denied Dutch, and she was my special cross because she took her handicap so cheerfully and remained so sweet under all provocations that she was constantly held up to me as an example and seemed to accentuate my own shortcomings. Poor Dutch had been carsick all the way, and both her clothes and Mamma's attested to the fact. Anyone near Dutch had no choice but to share in her violent outbursts of sickness.

Only the baby, a little over two, did credit to Papa. Called Pugsy, more in admiration than derision of her upturned little nose, she was the family beauty and fully cognizant of the fact. Soft blonde curls and wide-spaced eyes gave her an appeal that only I seemed to recognize as being carefully designed to get her more attention than I thought she needed. Because I was the one most often called upon to supply that attention, and because the one sure way to keep Pugsy entertained was to change her clothes, she arrived at our destination looking adorably immaculate.

Papa, who never saw anything in anyone's appearance to criticize, greeted us with the natural exuberance of a man who hadn't seen his family in a year. Each of us was given a bear hug and then passed on to complete strangers, who crowded each other to get a closer glimpse of this strange assortment of human nature, the women's faces registering horror, the men's amusement.

Papa, absorbed in his own happiness, saw none of this. Only Mamma saw, and she reacted as Mamma would. Lifting her small head haughtily, ignoring the outstretched hands reaching toward her, she said to Papa, "Well, Jim, where's that new house you've been bragging about? We can't get there too quick to suit me."

Someone explained that our furniture had just arrived and was not yet in place, and perhaps we'd better just stay with the church members that night. Mamma settled that quickly. "Thank you, we're staying at home. It won't take long to put up the beds."

Papa's buggy was waiting, but it had only a single seat. Mamma got in with him, taking Dutch and Pugsy, and leaving the rest of us to be parceled out among the members' rigs. Squeezed in between a fat couple, both of them large enough to shut off completely my view of the town, I found myself bombarded by questions I wasn't at all sure how to answer.

"So you folks come from Waco. I had an aunt lived there once. Do folks go barefoot there at your age? Seems like you're a pretty big girl not to wear shoes in public. How old are you? Ten, going on eleven? My, when I was that age I'd have died if somebody had caught me barefoot, even at home.

"What's your name? Ennen? Oh. Wherever did they find a name like Ennen? What are your little sisters' names? Dutch and Pugsy? Oh my, they must have other names. You say you don't even know? My, that's funny, a girl as big as you who don't even know her own sisters' names. Well, I must say that is funny."

By then I wasn't sure I knew my own name. Feeling utterly crushed, physically and mentally, I could think of nothing except a possible chance of escape. My mind was blank, my stomach was churning, and deep in my heart was planted the first seed of guilt. It was to grow into rank weeds while I lived in the limelight that was the trying place of every minister's family in a small American community.

Unaware of my reaction to her words, the woman rattled on. "Are those your best clothes? I must say we expected to see our pastor's family more dressed up—well, it's true, John, so why shouldn't I say it? You know the whole town will be judging our church by them."

The humiliating ride ended at last before the new parsonage, gleaming in fresh white paint and shining new shingles. Though it was no better than the Texas home we had left, it looked wonderful in comparison with the teepee lodge we had envisioned—the typical Indian home pictured in our geography book. Delightedly, I squirmed my way out of the narrow crevasse, climbed across the outraged fat woman, and sprinted inside.

Almost at once the house was overrun with people. In the midst of the confusion Mamma sat on a straight-backed chair, with a stony face that would have warned me even without the angry flash in her blue eyes. Pug sat in her lap, gloating over attention, and Dutch crowded against her with her grimy thumb in her mouth, while Papa repeated introductions he'd begun at the depot. "Easter, this is Sister Hinslow . . . and Sister Martin . . . and Sister Breeding."

"How do you do, Sister Reaves," each woman murmured in turn, offering Mamma a limp hand which she took and dropped quickly. Knowing all the storm signals, I stood and waited for the lightning to strike, my stomach churning in dread.

It came as suddenly as I'd known it would. When one of the women said brightly, "We'll just look over the house now, Sister Reaves. We're all terribly proud of it," she replied clearly, "It looks to me like you'd have come to look it over before we got here."

The house cleared quickly of visitors after that, the women not waiting until they were through the door before expressing their outrage. "Well, I never! Did you hear that? Poor Brother Reaves, I'm so sorry for him I could cry."

When I had shut the door on the last one, I turned back to see Mamma crying and saying much the same thing. "Oh, Jim, I'm sorry I said that, but I just couldn't help it. I'm afraid they'll blame you, and I don't want that. But why in the world did they have to come just now when we're all so tired and hungry and dirty?"

Papa put his arms about her and gave his classic reply that was to become standard for all such occasions, "Easter, honey, they're good people and they mean well."

I went in search of Rusty. He was sitting on the back steps, looking disgustedly at the bow and arrows over which he'd worked for weeks. "Gee whiz," he muttered as I sat down beside him, "somebody sure didn't know what they were talking about. Everybody said there'd be Indians up here, and I didn't see a one when we drove through town. Did you?"

"No," I said truthfully. Why go into details about how little I had seen? "People here all look just like people."

But he seemed so disappointed that my heart melted. "Maybe they live off in the hills or something and don't come to town unless they're ready to attack. Let's go ask Papa."

Papa found our question an amusing one. "The Indians in the Chickasaw Nation are all civilized," he explained. "They dress and live just like anyone. Did you see Sister Breeding today? She's a full-blood."

It was easy to remember Sister Breeding, an attractive brunette who wore a stylish dress trimmed with what looked like millions of tiny beads, and who had given Mamma what I took to be a commiserating, instead of a condemning, look as she left. But only God knew how disillusioning the recollection was.

9

Rusty's reaction was typical. He made a dive for my dress pocket, ripping it half off in his haste. "Gimme back my knife," he snapped, "and if you ever touch it again I'll wham you one."

Rusty, like Mamma, had to be understood.

2

Two mornings later Papa took us to school. Dutch and I clung to his big, horny hands for courage; the two boys trailed behind. The building was a two-story frame with six classrooms. In one corner of the playground was a one-room structure housing the high school, which meant the three grades above the sixth. The superintendent taught this group, leaving his classes when his presence was required to administer discipline in the other building.

None of us had expected the attention we attracted. Children left their games to crowd around us, shouting to each other, "It's Brother Reaves' kids!" The teachers inside heard the commotion and rushed out in a body, clamoring to know if Papa had one for them.

The school superintendent came to claim Red, who would be in the eighth grade. Dutch was claimed by a first-grade teacher and willingly relinquished Papa's hand. That left only Rusty and me, both of us overwhelmed by all the flattering attention.

The sixth-grade teacher made her first error with Rusty. "Oh, so this one will be mine. My, but isn't he the handsome one! All the girls will be crazy over you, young man."

11

I saw Rusty stiffen; then his eyes began turning inward, slowly but surely. Spreading his legs apart, he looked from the fawning teacher to the giggling children and announced belligerently, "I can lick any kid in school."

Shocked silence greeted this announcement. Then error number two, accompanied by a nervous laugh. "Oh, my, and you look so sweet. But you can't mean that, Rusty. Brother Reaves' son wouldn't——"

That did it. Rusty never ignored a challenge. His eyes, definitely crossed now, swept over the group around us, selecting the biggest boy present. In one quick lunge he whammed the boy in the stomach and kicked him on the shin. A second later the two were going after each other like ancient enemies, and it took the combined efforts of Papa and the teachers to separate them and restore peace.

Papa's humiliation and distress were pitiful. Though I could understand and share in his acute embarrassment, all my loyalty was for Rusty. That silly teacher shouldn't have said that about his looking so sweet. The last thing Rusty wanted was to be what he appeared to be at first glance. But how could an adult understand that?

At the first recess I filed out with the other pupils, then backed against the wall to brace myself for the overwhelming overtures of friendship. Dutch came flying straight to my side like a homing pigeon, grabbing my hand for encouragement. Together we stood there, defiant, unsmiling, facing an increasing number of giggling girls. After my humiliating experience with the fat woman the day we arrived, I didn't even question what the giggles were about. These, too, must find us "funny" and small credit to Papa and his church. It wasn't until an older girl stopped and whispered kindly, "Your little sister's shoes are on the wrong feet," that I had any idea the giggles were for some special reason.

12

Then I looked down, and horror rose in me. Dutch wore high button shoes, with the rows of shiny buttons on the inside of her ankles, her feet grotesquely ill-shapen. No wonder they all laughed.

My pride completely crushed, I bolted through the ring of giggling girls, dragging the protesting Dutch after me. Without any sense of direction, I headed for home.

We ran until Dutch began stumbling and crying. Then I slowed down, realizing we were lost in this frighteningly new place. But we didn't stay lost long. There were no inhibitions in Dutch. When she cried, she cried—and very soon we were again surrounded, this time by women who ran out from the houses as I tried to drag Dutch past them. Someone recognized us and took us within sight of the parsonage.

Mamma was unimpressed with my trouble. "For pity's sake, child, why didn't you just change the shoes for her?"

Such a simple solution hadn't even occurred to me. But how could I explain to Mamma how ridicule or criticism affected me? She and Rusty would have gotten angry and put everyone in her place. My reaction was a paralysis of all power of thought or action, leaving me a quivering mass of injured feelings. This egocentric pride made me vulnerable and created problems wherever I went. It brought its own punishment that day, when I had to return to school to explain my absence as best I could, and also explain to Dutch's teacher that she had been so exhausted when I got her home that Mamma put her to bed.

When school was dismissed that afternoon I lingered, looking about in sick dread for Rusty. When I heard excited yells and saw the group of boys on their side of the grounds, I knew I had located him. Whenever there was a fight going on I could trust Rusty to be in the thick of it. Sure enough, he and the boy he had attacked without provocation were finish ing what Rusty had begun. They left the grounds arm in arm and apparently the best of friends. But Rusty still would have to account for his torn shirt and bloodied nose, and neither Papa nor Mamma would treat the matter as lightly as did the subject of his unprovoked attack, and the realization made me ill.

This sickening sensation of dread became a familiar emotion to me during the next several years. I couldn't hear or see a disturbance on the school grounds without visualizing Rusty's crossed eyes and clenched fists in the midst of it. He wasn't always there; but I always dreaded that he might be, and he usually was.

I used to go home in dread, too, my mind busily framing excuses and alibis for Rusty. Sometimes my defense was ill-timed and premature and brought on the trouble I wanted to spare him. But more often than not Papa had already heard about the latest set-to, and no amount of cunning on either my part or Rusty's was able to save him from a session with Mamma and Papa. Before the first month had past he was known all over town as Parson Reaves' wild kid, and such fame has its price.

Red, by nature more serious and responsible, soon came to share in Rusty's reputation, for he had a fierce loyalty that wouldn't let him stand by and see Rusty battling alone. He usually joined in without having any idea what the fight was about, and very often undertook later to give Rusty a licking for being so eager to fight.

Poor Papa, who hated violence and recognized no possible excuse or provocation for it, was driven to the point of despair at this incomprehensible wildness in his sons. Night after night he administered the punishment he felt to be most effective. Calling the culprits into his study, he'd make them kneel while he prayed that God would forgive their sins and bring repentance to their hearts. Because he spared neither God nor child any details of the sin they'd committed, and because the floor was hard and bare and often the sinners had not yet had supper, repentance usually came without too much delay. But the fights went on, in spite of much more drastic punishment administered by the superintendent, who believed in applying a big paddle to the appropriate place while he prayed. That this superintendent was also one of Papa's deacons complicated things a little for Rusty.

But there came a day when even Papa's patience was exhausted. That was when he caught Rusty slyly reading a forbidden Nick Carter book while Papa told God about his sins and begged forgiveness for him. Papa rose in his wrath then, and it was something terrible to see. Grabbing Rusty by the scruff of his neck, he dragged him into the kitchen, where Mamma and I were preparing supper.

"See that?" Papa roared, pointing to the broom standing in the corner. "The very next fight you get into, I'm going to whale you with that broom handle. I'm tired of having folks stop me on the street to ask me if I know what bad children I've got."

Thrusting the Nick Carter book into the fire box, Papa added another ultimatum. "And no more bringing such trash as this into my house, either. You've got all the reading material you need in your schoolbooks and your Sunday-school lesson."

Rusty set up a howl of protest. "I borrowed that book from Bill Blake!"

"I don't care where you got it. Bill Blake and you are both better off with it burned up. Maybe you'll find time now to do a little studying. Brother Olsen tells me your grades are awful. I tell you, Easter, these boys have got to straighten up. Why, I'm getting so I can't preach for thinking about how everybody must be looking at my own family and wondering why I don't do something about them."

When Papa used that tone of voice, the very walls trembled. For a while there was a pseudo peace in the parsonage.

Then one day Rusty borrowed Red's bicycle, bought with money he'd earned picking cotton, without getting Red's permission. Because he'd left it with a flat tire the last time he'd used it, Red started out in pursuit, with blood in his eye.

A half-hour later a man stopped to tell Papa his two sons were murdering each other a few blocks away. He'd tried to separate them but without success. "They're so bloody I couldn't tell one from the other, Parson Reaves."

Papa stalked into the kitchen and picked up the broom. "I'll separate them," he told Mamma, and the very quietness of his grim voice struck terror into my heart.

A little while later Red and Rusty stumbled into the kitchen, groping for the water and towels we had waiting for them. Their faces were bloody, their clothes dirty and torn, but they didn't appear at all angry with each other. And Papa, following with the broom, looked more bewildered than anything else.

"Now," Papa said, taking a firm grip on the broom handle and planting himself in front of the two warriors, "I want to know what all this is about. Brother Dawson said you were fighting each other, but I find you fighting together against four other boys. Red, what started it this time?"

Red spit out some blood, fingered a loose tooth, and managed a sick grin. "Well, it was like this, Papa. I told Rusty I'd skin his hide off if he ever touched my bicycle again. I found him down there letting those boys ride around the block for a nickel apiece. So I lit into him."

He stopped to spit out more blood, then went on sheepishly,

16

"Well, I just about had Rusty ready to yell quits when those other four boys took sides with him and pitched into me."

Tightening his grip on the broom, Papa looked accusingly at Rusty. "You mean you actually let your brother have to fight five at once?"

"No, sir," Rusty said promptly. "Soon's they pitched in to help me I started fighting on Red's side. And did we knock their stupid heads together good! I bet——"

"That will do," Papa roared. "Rusty, I don't know what I'm going to do with you."

Poor Papa looked appealingly at Mamma, who just went over and took the broom out of his hand and began sweeping up water the boys had spilled in their haste. "Take them in the study and pray over them," she said calmly. "But don't forget to tell God that the boys stuck together like brothers should."

That was one thing you could be sure of—the Reaves sinners always stuck together.

3

Papa finished his supper and pushed back his chair. "Easter, are you ready for prayer meeting? It's almost time to start."

It was the first Wednesday night after our arrival at the parsonage, and Mamma looked tired enough to drop. Thinking of all she had done that day, of the window-washing and the scrubbing and the carpet laid in the parlor, I couldn't blame her when she said flatly, "I'm not going."

Obviously upset, Papa tried diplomacy. "Hon, it won't look right if you don't go. The members expect to see you. Ennen can put the children to bed and do the dishes."

"Ennen can go to prayer meeting if anybody has to go," Mamma said acidly. "I'm going to bed, and the dishes can stand till morning."

I looked at Mamma suspiciously. She abhorred letting dirty dishes stand, and no matter how tired she might be she never, never went to bed and left her kitchen untidy.

Papa, too, realized something was wrong. He said uneasily, "Honey, are you sick?"

"Yes, I am," she snapped. "I'm sick of folks staring at me and whispering behind their hands and taking me apart with their eyes. I had enough Sunday to do me. I'm just not going over there tonight for more."

Papa seldom argued when Mamma used that tone, but now he said pleadingly, "They're good folks, Easter. They just have to get used to you."

Even I knew at once that he'd said the wrong thing. Mamma's eyes were blue fire as she got up from the table. "Nobody has to get used to me," she said scathingly. "They can just let me alone and that will suit me fine. Do you know that two of your good sisters came here today to tell me that very thing? That fat Mrs. Hinslow and another woman had the crust to come here and virtually tell me I had to go to prayer meeting tonight. Even demanded that I bring all the children so they could look them over again. Just what do they think we are—public property? If they bought us with what they pay you, then they sure got us all cheap, that's all I've got to say. Except that I'll go to church when I want to and not because I'm told to."

Having delivered that speech, Mamma marched off to bed, shooing the protesting little girls in front of her. I began gathering up the dishes, for once eager for the job I ordinarily shirked. Papa stopped me by saying sternly, "Let the dishes alone, like she said, Ennen. You can't all stay away tonight."

For a moment I debated appealing to Mamma. She wouldn't, I felt, require me to do what she had refused to do herself. But Papa added an appeal that touched my heart. "I don't want them to get the wrong idea about all of you, daughter."

Sensing that he was thinking about Rusty and the three fights he'd already had at school, as well as about Mamma's unfriendly attitude, I was moved by a compassion rare for me. Putting away the butter, I meekly walked out with him, leaving the table just as it was.

Only a vacant lot separated the parsonage from the church.

19

At once I saw from the teams everywhere that we were late. The church was well filled already, and every head turned in unison to stare at Papa and me as we entered. Shrinking inwardly from that battery of eyes, I felt the dubious exaltation of a martyr as I followed Papa down the aisle to a seat near the front. This, I thought smugly, should win me a few favors from Mamma.

Sunday, our first in the church, had been pretty awful for all of us, unaccustomed to the limelight as we were. Papa had been preaching only a few years, and before leaving us to come to the Indian Territory he had been something of a roving missionary, doing evangelistic work for the Texas Baptist Home Mission Board. Because this was his first pastorate, his family had never had a part in his church life and none of us was prepared for the proprietary interest these people seemed to take in us. So it was something of a shock when Professor Olsen took it upon himself to ask us all to come to the pulpit platform and be individually introduced at the beginning of the Sunday service.

Since the platform was a good two feet higher than the floor level, we had felt very conspicuous and awkward as we lined up for inspection. Mamma said after we got home that she had fully expected someone to come up and examine her ears to see if they were clean. Certainly we felt the critical eyes of the audience didn't miss anything unless it was the area back of our ears.

Pugsy put a quick end to the ordeal for all of us. Papa gallantly offered to take her out of Mamma's arms, and Pugsy made violent objections. After all, she barely knew the strange man we'd come to live with, since she'd been just an infant when he left. So he only made matters worse by attempting to placate her with a kiss planted on her round cheek. Grabbing a handful of mustache with one hand while the palm of the other tried to flatten his nose against his face, she gave screaming voice to her indignation.

In the resulting confusion, before Papa relinquished the yelling child to Mamma, Red and Rusty escaped, and I resorted to hysterical giggling. Only Dutch maintained her poise. As Mamma hurriedly left the platform with Pugsy, with me close on her heels, Dutch lingered and faced the audience undaunted. "I'm Dutch," she announced, loud and calm—the only introduction that actually took place. We all felt the resulting laughter that swept through the church wasn't alone for her.

No wonder Mamma hadn't wanted to go back, I thought miserably, feeling the eyes boring right into my spine. I could only guess that a part of poor Mamma's embarrassment had been caused by the fact that none of our clothes could bear very close inspection that Sunday. She hadn't had time to press the wrinkles out of our dresses, and hers was her second best and not as immaculately clean as Mamma liked her clothes to be. Her one good dress had been worn on the train and still bore odors reminiscent of Dutch.

This midweek service, known as prayer meeting, was mercifully short. The instant Papa pronounced the benediction, a voice from behind me whispered in my ear, "Little girl, where's your mother tonight?"

The intense interest echoing in the voice alerted me even before I turned to face eyes bright with excitement. I said cautiously, "In bed. She's got a headache." Quick alibis were my only real talent.

"Run quick and wake her up," the voice said. "All the folks are coming over directly to give her a pounding."

Terror lent swiftness to my thin legs. In a flash I was out of the church and across the yard, bursting into Mamma's room to wake her from a sound sleep. "Get up quick and

21

hide," I panted. "The church people are coming over to give you a beating."

Mamma sat up in bed to stare at me in unbelief. "A beating? Child, what are you talking about?"

Breathlessly I repeated the woman's words, but before I'd finished Mamma was up and snatching at her clothes. "Hurry, child," she panted, struggling to pin up her long hair and dress at the same time. "Help me straighten up things. Make the beds, get the girls up and dress them. Oh, they would have to pick a night when things were all topsy-turvy."

We hurried, with no time to ask or answer questions. I still didn't know what might be going to happen, but Mamma's excitement carried no alarm. When Dutch stubbornly refused to wake up, I dragged her out of bed and dressed her while she slept on her feet. This proved such an exhausting task that I simply couldn't cope with Pugsy. When she began to show violent objections, I just pushed her down between the down pillows and yanked the heavy bedspread over her. When the covers were all smoothed you couldn't tell little Pugsy was even there, and I knew Mamma was too upset to miss her.

Somehow we got the beds made and surplus clothes pushed out of sight. Mamma's shaking hands were sticking pins in her hair when the front door burst open and Papa stood there, belatedly attempting to warn Mamma. "Easter, it's a pounding——"

Before the words were out of his mouth they were all in the house, everyone loaded with sacks and bundles of varying sizes. The women were silent and nervous, but the men all made a lot of fuss, yelling things about Mamma being pounded because she didn't look as well fed as Papa. Somebody asked the way to the kitchen, and Mamma darted me a look of pure horror that told me she was thinking the same thing I was. All those dirty dishes, the cluttered dining-room table! In

22

our efforts to straighten up the bedroom, neither of us had thought of the kitchen.

A woman, having caught that look between Mamma and me, grabbed my arm and pushed me toward the dining-room door, opening off the front room. A lamp left burning in the kitchen by the boys revealed the mess on the table. "Quick," the woman whispered—I had just time to recognize the ample Mrs. Hinslow—"get your dish pan."

While I scurried toward the kitchen, she planted herself in the doorway, blocking it completely and talking as volubly as I remembered she could. She was still there, holding back the crowd, when I pushed the pan of dishes into the oven, a trick I had learned when I wanted to postpone my chore without attracting Mamma's attention.

When she saw my mission was accomplished, Mrs. Hinslow called out jovially, "Why don't you all bring those groceries to the dining room? And where's those cakes we mean to cut?"

The crowd surged into the dining room, and Mamma's relief at seeing the cleared table was pathetic. But, looking at her in the light of the lamp Papa brought in, I saw another reason to feel sick horror. In her haste Mamma had gotten into the handiest dress, the same one she had worn at her house-cleaning tasks all day. The spotted front bore mute evidence of her earlier activities, and I knew poor Mamma would just die when she realized how she must look to others.

Again Mrs. Hinslow saved the day. Almost before Papa had set the lamp down she was whispering in my ear, "Hasn't your mamma got a clean apron? Get it and slip it around her."

It took only a minute to get the apron from the china-cabinet drawer. Then I slipped behind Mamma while the fat good Samaritan blocked her from view, and the soiled dress disappeared behind a freshly starched apron.

While my shaking hands fumbled with the apron strings

I heard Mrs. Hinslow whisper to Mamma, "Don't be upset, Sister Reaves. Surprises always catch you with your pants down, so to speak. I was worried it might be that way is why we came over today to make sure you'd all be at prayer meeting. You know, already fixed up, so to speak."

About then a girl, whom I remembered having seen at school because she stuck her tongue out at me every time I looked across the room, edged over to make friendly overtures. "My name's Trudy Wilson. What's yours?"

Feeling she already knew the answer, I supplied it nevertheless. Her reaction was what I expected. "Ennen," she repeated condescendingly. "I never heard of a name like that. Why didn't your folks name you something pretty?"

All my young life I'd wondered about that same thing. My unusual name was my hair shirt. What child wanted a name, coined especially for her, that no one else ever had? Suddenly the shirt was so prickly I found myself telling one of the small white lies, if lies are ever small and white, for which I had already won dubious fame in my family.

"I've got a pretty middle name," I fibbed. "Sometimes I'm called by that."

'What is it?" Her skeptical tone demanded proof and so I plunged in deeper.

"Beatrice."

Actually it didn't seem like a lie just then. Beatrice had been my secret name for myself for a long time, displacing the despised middle name that was even more of a cross than Ennen. What possible glamour was there in a name like Browne? But take Beatrice . . .

Trudy accepted it, duly impressed—so much so that she had to find another way of showing her superiority. "This isn't your house," she said. "It's just as much mine as yours because it belongs to the church."

24

Then she proceeded to give weight to her words by going from room to room and opening bureau drawers and peering into such sacred places as Mamma's chest-type trunk that her grandmother had brought over from Germany as a bride. None of us ever opened Mamma's trunk or Mamma's bureau drawers. In our household, the sacredness of personal property was a law that we respected. But what could I do except follow her about helplessly? That small lie called Beatrice had put me in Trudy's power.

Someone came along munching cake, and Trudy lost interest in her new property. "Come on," she cried. "They're cutting the cake."

I was right at her heels when she got back to the dining room, where some women were slicing a glossy chocolate cake and one piled high with shredded coconut.

Trudy accepted a large slice from the woman serving the coconut, but I looked longingly at the other one. "Chocolate, please." Chocolate was my weakness.

The woman serving the chocolate gave an odd glance of triumph at the one behind the white cake. But just as her knife measured off a huge slice, Trudy whispered in my ear, "Take coconut." I started to shake my head, but she saw the refusal coming. "You'd better—Beatrice."

Maybe it wasn't blackmail, but how could I know? Swallowing painfully, I tore my eyes away from that glossy dark surface and said hastily, "I guess I'll take coconut." The cake gagged me.

Trudy, having consumed her second piece, announced proudly, "My mother baked the coconut. She makes a lot better cake than Mrs. Baker with her old chocolate."

Later we learned that the rivalry between Mrs. Wilson and Mrs. Baker extended beyond the culinary department. Mrs. Wilson was the church organist, and she demanded constant reassurance that her job was more vital to the welfare of the church than that held by Mrs. Baker, president of the Ladies' Aid Society. But Mrs. Baker was quite sure that the very blood of the church depended upon the Ladies' Aid, and she *was* the Ladies' Aid.

While the cake-serving was still going on, excitement broke out in the bedroom. Someone sat down on our bed without knowing that Pugsy lay under those carefully smoothed covers. When they heard her crunch or something, they jerked the spread back, and there was little Pugsy under the pillow, practically breathing her last. Her round cheeks were purple, her mouth gaping like a fish out of water. With a scream that brought the crowd running into the bedroom, a woman snatched up the child and began pounding her on the back and blowing breath into her lungs.

Fortunately, Pugsy had strong lungs. A moment or so later she was loudly demonstrating that fact, comforted by Mamma, who kept saying that she didn't understand why Pugsy had got back into bed. For some time the small queen of our household was the center of attention, and for once that suited me thoroughly. Well I knew that once it shifted from her it might well focus on me, the cause of it all.

Mentally I was scurrying about trying to find a better excuse for burying poor Pugsy alive than the trite one of her resistance to being dressed, when excitement appeared to be transferred again to the dining room. Welcoming a change, I edged my way in to see what had caused my reprieve.

It was Dutch this time. She sat on the floor with an empty plate in front of her, fairly bulging with coconut cake. What she hadn't eaten was scattered all around her. Dutch was very partial to coconut.

There were loud guffaws from the men, a few titters from the women. I shivered inwardly, for I saw the outrage in Mrs. Wilson's face.

Dutch saved herself, as she had an uncanny knack of doing. She stood up, rubbing one hand across her stomach in genuine satisfaction, as she fairly purred, "That was sure awful good coconut cake."

No one could resist Dutch's smile. Mrs. Wilson relaxed and patted Dutch's brown head. "You're a very smart little girl," she said. Then, turning to the others, she announced in Dutch's own dulcet tones, "Well, it looks like the rest of you will have to eat chocolate now."

Mrs. Baker spoiled her *coup de grâce.* "Oh no they don't," she snapped, snatching up the less-than-half-eaten cake. "I wouldn't think of making anybody suffer."

With that she marched out, holding the cake in front of her. Others soon followed, and after the house was emptied of the self-invited party guests I looked at the cake-strewn floor and waited in dread for Mamma's explosion. But Mamma, I found, was looking over the dining-room table, almost buried under a small mountain of groceries, her eyes bright with tears.

"I never saw as much food in our house at one time in all my life," she said, her voice shaking a little. "And just to think that this very day I was worried half sick about how we were ever going to manage, with no money and nothing in the house to eat, hardly."

It was a lot of food—several bags of flour, a hundred-pound sack of sugar, a ten-gallon pail of lard, a tow sack of potatoes, a side of bacon, two hams, coffee, canned goods of all kinds, and jars and jars of homemade pickles, jellies, and preserves; even an untouched cake, a loaf of homemade bread, and a shoe box of delicious-looking cookies that were fast disappearing with Red's and Rusty's help.

Awe filled me as I looked the assortment over, then turned a puzzled face to Mamma. "Why do they call this a beating?"

"A pounding," Mamma corrected me, smiling. "I guess it got

its name from the fact that when the idea started, people were supposed to take a pound of something. But just look at this." She made a sweeping gesture that included all the table, too excited to even notice what the boys were doing to the cookies. "Why, some of these people must have brought a hundred pounds of something instead of one pound."

Papa, grinning broadly, put his arm about her. "Easter, I told you these were good people."

Mamma said meekly, "I guess you're right, Jim. They must be. Do you know something? That Mrs. Hinslow and Mrs. Breeding didn't come today to make it their business that I go to prayer meeting, like I thought. They were just afraid I'd be caught in a dirty dress and with the house in a mess, which was just what I was and I guess it served me right."

Such meekness from Mamma was startling. It was almost a relief to have her add, a moment later, "My stars! The fuss those silly women make over who bakes the best cake. Jim, how am I ever going to learn to say and do the right thing without making somebody mad?"

Papa, the saint, had his answer on the tip of his tongue. "We'll ask God's help, honey. He knows what's in people's hearts and what they need to have said to them."

It was a further relief to have Mamma forget, in her mellowed mood, that Pugsy couldn't have gotten under those smooth covers by herself.

4

The proud Baptists liked to brag that their church-owned parsonage was completely modern. Since the term is a relative one, it doubtless was, measured by the standards of frontier living. To be modern in 1900 in the Indian Territory simply meant to have a sink in the kitchen, with a hand pump that brought in water after a little priming and coaxing and back-bending effort. A sturdy soap box, kept handy for that purpose, raised my height to where I could get proper leverage on the iron handle, and the reward of seeing the stream of water gush out of the pump spout justified any effort involved.

Our water was brought in from a cistern on the back porch, so it was especially desirable because it was soft, making laundry work much easier for Mamma. A drainage pipe carried the used water out into the yard, but because it ended near the house Mamma never would let us empty washbasins or dish pans into the sink. They had to be dumped into a disreputable large bucket called a slop bucket, and when it was full it was either carried outside to be used around trees or flowers or, if we were keeping hogs, to be poured into the trough in the pigpen. Nothing ever went to waste around Mamma, descendant of thrifty German ancestors—certainly nothing as precious as water, used or otherwise.

But to back up their claim to modern thinking, the planners of the parsonage had included a small room that opened onto the back porch and that was politely called the bathroom. It had nothing at all in it by way of plumbing attachments, but it bore mute evidence of the community's faith in the day when running water would be a civic achievement. However, it did provide privacy for Papa and the boys for their Saturday night baths, leaving the kitchen for the rest of us.

The small room also made a good place for Mamma to pile dirty clothes to await wash day, which was usually Friday at the parsonage, for two good reasons. One was the fact that by doing laundry at the end of the week our limited supply of clothing was clean for Sunday's wear; the other was that the rinse water could be saved and used for Saturday's scrubbing. That saved not only water but also effort at the pump.

So Friday was a day to be dreaded, for I could be sure of finding the noon dishes unwashed when I got home from school, maybe the beds unmade, and a general state of confusion and disorder. Mamma would still be bending over the washtubs, on the back porch in mild weather, in the kitchen if it was bad. In winter the house would reek with the smell of soapsuds, for our soap was the homemade lye variety that carried a pungent odor. If Papa was home, he would be lying in wait for each of us to make sure we did our share to get the clothes on the lines and the tubs emptied, so that the delayed supper preparations could be started.

No day was ever long enough for Mamma to do the weekly laundry alone, for the process involved in making clothes clean by pre-Machine Age methods was tedious, to say the least. Unless the weather was too bad, the boys started wash day before they left for school by building a wood fire in the yard, under the big black pot, which they filled with water and shavings of strong lye soap. As soon as Mamma got us all off to school, she began her meticulous job of rubbing every inch of every garment or piece of linen over the corrugated surface of a copper washboard. This took hours, for no smallest surface could be overlooked, and seven people, plus innumerable guests, could use a lot of clothes and household linens.

After all traces of grime were removed, the white things were dropped into the pot of soapsuds to boil. Nothing that escaped this actual boiling process was considered sanitary, and even light-colored things must be "scalded"—brought to the point of boiling. During this cooking process the clothes must be punched every few minutes with a sawed-off broomstick, to make sure each particle got well under the steaming suds. Since there was supposed to be added cleansing power in these punches, Mamma's clothes got many extra licks.

After the boiling process, each piece was lifted into a tub, with enough cold water added to make them cool enough to handle. Then the rubbing process was repeated, though perhaps with a little less meticulous care this time. Next, each piece must be lifted and swished and lifted and swished in a tub of rinsing water, wrung out, and dropped into another tub of water into which bluing had been put to insure whiteness. When the wash was heavy, Mamma's clothes often got two rinsings in addition to the bluing. Surely only women who have lived through those scrub-board and hand-wringing days can appreciate the mechanized age in which we live.

Every day was ironing day at the parsonage, for the basket seldom got emptied before it was filled again. The heavy sadirons stood on the kitchen range all the time, ready for use whenever Mamma found any time free from other household duties. Ironing the flat linens was my job, and how I hated those sheets that must be folded and unfolded and folded again, never seeming to come out quite even.

Seldom did the kitchen range get cold, for if there wasn't a meal in preparation there might be bread baking, which had to be done several times a week, or ironing or extra baking, or maybe soap or jelly making. It almost seemed as if the natural setting for Mamma's slight figure was that ugly background of black metal.

It required much attention, that big wood range, much cooperative effort on the part of all. Red split the wood that fed its insatiable appetite. Rusty's job was to keep the big box behind the stove filled with firewood and kindling, and trouble awaited him if he stayed out too late or forgot his nightly chore. My task was to keep the reservoir tank at the end of the stove filled with water, and it was amazing how fast that water could be dipped out or just evaporate.

Papa, who made the first fire in the morning, assumed the obligation of emptying the ash pan, but that didn't mean it was Papa's task alone, for usually there was a wide trail of ashes across Mamma's spotless kitchen, or a little heap beside the stove, waiting to be swept up. And a goodly portion of every Saturday morning had to be spent in thoroughly cleaning the big range, inside and out. The oven must be scrubbed, soot raked out from under it, nickel trimmings polished until they shone. Yet in spite of all the man-hours of work it demanded from us, it was always a warm and friendly object, exuding delicious odors and greeting us with the cheery singing of the big iron teakettle or the bright crackle of flames.

Another chore that fell to my lot was keeping the lamps filled and the chimneys cleaned. Rusty was supposed to help with filling the lamps, since Papa bought kerosene in five-gallon cans, which were too heavy for me to manage alone. If Rusty didn't show up in time, there was no way to protect him, for usually my awkward attempts to manage without help left telltale oil spots on the back porch.

Because kerosene was no small item on a preacher's limited budget, we seldom burned more than one lamp at a time except for the wall lamps in the kitchen, which were never blown out until the house was made dark for the night. Of course each room had its lamp, the one in the parlor having an ornate shade with flowers and leaves painted on it. But for studying and reading after supper, we all gathered about the dining table, in the center of which was our tallest and brightest lamp. Mamma brought her sewing or mending and Papa read his Bible or worked on a sermon, while practice in spelling, reading, or arithmetic went on. Mamma was never too busy to help any of us with our lessons, and she had an unlimited and inexhaustible fund of knowledge in spite of the fact that she herself had never gone beyond the fifth grade. On Saturday nights all of us from Red to Pugsy prepared our Sunday-school lessons. The smaller girls were drilled in memory verses, and we older kids took turns reading the text in the Bible.

Every evening concluded with the family altar hour, when Papa read a chapter from the Bible and prayed. We never minded the reading because Papa became so engrossed that he didn't notice if we quietly continued with our lessons or drew pictures or passed each other notes. But the praying was another matter.

Prayer, to Papa, was a ritual that demanded kneeling. The uncovered floor was hard, and cold in the winter. Papa's prayers were long and often very personal if there had been any matter of discipline that day. And the more personal they were, the longer.

If Rusty was close to me, he sometimes took advantage of my forced discretion to yank my hair, tickle me in the ribs, or pinch me. Often my giggling aloud at such times won a bonus session for us after the others had gone to bed. Once, I remember, I outraged poor Papa by falling sound asleep while he prayed for me because of my irreverence.

Among the conveniences of our 1900 parsonage was an outhouse, which also did credit to the church in that it had a shingle roof, a compact floor, and a tight door that insured complete privacy. This door was secured on the inside by a metal hook and on the outside by a big wooden button. Woe to the one caught leaving that outside button off after a visit inside. Mamma kept chickens, and they had little respect for her ironbound rule that the outhouse be kept immaculately clean.

The small structure had three seats, two large and one small, each complete with hinged covers. The covers hadn't been there when we took over the parsonage—they had been one of Mamma's first demands for improvements. Woe again to the outhouse visitor who failed to close the lids and to use a generous shovelful of wood ashes kept in a box in the corner, providing Mamma could trace the negligence to its proper source.

For reasons of health, rather than convenience, the outhouse was always as far as possible from the dwelling. Ours stood beside the small cowshed on the back of the lot and was reached by a well-worn path that skirted the garden. On cold or rainy days this path seemed very long and hazardous, especially if we had delayed too long in starting or if the call came after dark. This invariably happened with Dutch and Pugsy and, since neither could be expected to go alone, it fell to my lot to take them.

The night trips were what I hated, for like most imaginative children I had a secret fear of the dark. For me it was peopled

34

with dragons, and carrying Papa's lantern did little, I felt, but betray our presence. Always there was that black emptiness waiting when I tremblingly opened the door, and always Things lurked in the blackness outside while I vainly tried to hurry a stubborn child into starting the homeward journey back to the safety of the house.

Phlegmatic little Dutch could never be hurried. No matter how cold the night, she'd sit there with all the dignity of a queen on her throne, indifferent to the cold wind whistling about her bare buttocks and unmindful of threats or cajolery from me.

Pugsy presented a slightly different problem. She was frankly afraid of the dark and didn't care who knew it. Before I could lift her onto the little seat she had changed her mind and was ready to go back, pronto. Because I knew she would no sooner get inside than she'd demand to be taken again, I had to spend time persuading Pugsy that nature would cooperate if she would just sit a little longer.

It was useless to try to persuade my small sisters to go before night fell. They still set up a clamor after supper, especially if it was raining. Neither, it seemed to me, wanted to miss an opportunity to slosh through the mud of that path on a rainy night. And virtually never would they consent to go together, thus making one trip do for both.

All too often Dutch made her demands on me after the house was dark, even though I'd made sure she went just before going to bed. It took a great deal of sisterly affection to crawl out of warm covers in the middle of a cold night and go outside barefoot and clad only in a nightgown. More affection than I had, no doubt, for I usually went in a most rebellious frame of mind, knowing that an appeal to Mamma would only bring a statement with which I could not argue: "For heaven's sake, Ennen, if the child has to go she has to go."

The quickest way to take care of the late nocturnal calls,

I learned, was to lead Dutch quietly to the back porch and set her down on the edge, thus sparing our feet contact with the frosty ground. But this required exact estimating in the total dark. Too near the edge, and she took a four-foot fall into the rosebushes Mamma had brought with her from Texas. Too far back, and Mamma's sharp eyes might detect signs that would give me away. It worked during the worst of the winter but failed when spring came, bringing new growth to the rose-bushes. One night I miscalculated and Dutch went over. Her screams brought the whole family to her rescue, and it took the combined efforts of Papa and Red to extricate her from the rosebush and the combined efforts of Mamma and me to extricate the thorns from her anatomy.

After that, we either trod the garden path all the way or stopped at a safe distance from the house.

Dutch and I always headed straight for the kitchen when we got home from school, for usually Mamma was there, either ironing or at the stove. But one day toward the end of our second week at the parsonage we found no one in the kitchen but Pugsy, sitting flat on the floor with the butter dish in her lap. One finger had already carried most of a freshly churned pound of butter into her mouth, and she was still working on the rest. Butter was Pugsy's weakness. She ate it like candy when afforded the opportunity.

Snatching the butter dish away from her and setting it out of her reach, I asked where Mamma was. Her reply was a howl of angry protest that brought Papa out of his study, holding a book in which his finger marked his place.

"Mamma went to the Ladies' Aid," he said, fairly shouting to make himself heard. "She said for you to wash the dishes and look after the girls. What happened to her?"

I explained about the butter, but Papa was impatient to get back to his study. "I don't suppose it will hurt her," he said. "Give it back to her. I can't work with that noise."

Something told me Mamma wasn't going to like it, but Papa was still enough of a stranger that I stood a little in awe of him. So I gave the butter back to Pugsy, and she rewarded me with a baleful glare of triumph. "Injun mean," she declared. She'd called me that ever since she'd heard us talking about the possibility of going to the "Injun" Territory, finding it easier to say than Ennen. Pugsy always did things the easy way.

Dutch announced triumphantly, "I'm gonna tell Mamma," but that had too familiar a ring to notice. Dutch was always looking for something to tell Mamma.

As we crossed the dining room to the bedroom to change from the school dresses that would need to be worn again at least another day, our footsteps seemed to set up a hollow echo all over the house. Nothing was right with Mamma away. I couldn't remember ever before getting home from school to find her gone.

Dawdling over the lunch dishes she had left for me to do, I heard Mamma come in the front way, heard Dutch's shrill greeting. "Mamma, Ennen let Pugsy eat up all the butter."

Mamma came to the kitchen door, her blue eyes registering horror at sight of Pugsy's grease-smeared figure. "My stars alive! Just look at her dress. And even in her hair. Ennen, what on earth were you thinking about?"

I began to place the blame on Papa, but Dutch interrupted me. "You gave it to her. I saw you. Didn't she give it to you, Pugsy?"

Pugsy pushed back her curls with a greasy hand and nodded. "Injun gave it to me."

Two against one were odds that aroused all my fighting instincts. "But Papa said to!" I yelled, swinging the dripping dishrag in a wild arc toward Dutch's round face. "You know he said to!"

Mamma caught the dishrag with one hand as her other

hand connected with my face. "I don't care who said to!" she snapped. "You knew it would make her sick. Besides, what do you think we're going to do about butter for supper?"

That part hadn't bothered me, for I seldom ate butter. But Mamma's solution to her problem disturbed me greatly. "All right, young lady, you can just get busy and churn some more."

I hated churning. Usually that was Rusty's chore, for Red milked and fed the two cows we kept. But for almost an hour that night I stood pulling the dasher up and letting it fall—up, down, up, down—until it seemed my thin arms would pull out of their sockets. But the pain between my shoulder blades was nothing compared to the pain in my heart as I meditated on the injustice of life and the sweetness of revenge.

By the time the butter had come I had done such a thorough job of feeling sorry for myself that I didn't want any supper. Neither did Pugsy, oddly enough. Perhaps Mamma relented a little, for she said that I could take Pugsy and go to bed and Rusty could wash the dishes.

Undressing Pugsy, I had my chance at revenge. It was easy to catch a button on her flaxen curls and yank, and her yell of anguish did my heart good.

Then all I had to do was wait for Dutch to come to bed, pretend sleep until she was between the covers, and rake my big toenail viciously down the back of her leg. But Dutch recognized vengeance when she saw it. Her howls brought Mamma and Papa both to the bed, and she lost no time in giving her version of the incident. "Ennen scratched me on purpose! She did it on purpose, I know she did!"

One look at the evidence and I was in for it. "Ennen, just look at that awful scratch on the child's leg. Did you do that on purpose?"

It wasn't altogether respect for the truth that made me answer truthfully. What good was revenge if Dutch didn't know it as such? "She told a lie on me," I said surlily.

"I did not I did not I did not," Dutch chanted shrilly. "You gave the butter to Pugsy because I saw you do it."

Now was my moment of vindication, I thought. Breathlessly I waited for Papa to assume full blame for the crime I'd been charged with, but apparently he had no idea of what it was all about. He just looked at Mamma, his face filled with distress. "Easter, why do they all quarrel so much? I declare, I don't know what to do with them."

"I do," Mamma said grimly, yanking the covers back so they wouldn't interfere with her duty. After vigorously applying her hand to the proper part of my anatomy, she issued a warning we both knew better than to ignore. "One more peep out of either of you and I'm coming back in here and whip you both."

That made it simple to ease my wounded feelings. What could Dutch do when she got the second rake but whimper softly in her pillow? "Just yell," I whispered. "I just dare you to yell."

At that, Dutch was asleep sometime before I was. I lay awake a long while, thinking what unfeeling creatures fathers were and wishing we had never come here to live with Papa. In my eyes, he had betrayed me. How could I know that Papa hadn't even noticed what it was he had told me to give to Pugsy? A ten-year-old cannot understand an adult's abstractions, but injustice rankles deeply. That night I decided Papa was my enemy.

5

The next morning Mamma had forgotten the butter and the toenail-raking incidents in her absorption with the Ladies' Aid, about which she told Papa while we ate breakfast.

"I'm not going any more," she said flatly. "All they did was talk about everyone who wasn't there. I didn't know anyone to talk about, so I might as well have been at home where I belonged."

Her news delighted me but seemed to disturb Papa. "Easter, you'll have to go. They all expect you to. After all, the Ladies' Aid does a lot to help a pastor."

"Yes," Mamma said sharply. "They're planning now to do something to raise some of your back pay. Do you know what? They're going to have a pie supper next Saturday night. They voted that today."

Papa looked pleased as he forked another thick slice of bacon onto his plate. "Well, now, that's nice. We can certainly use some of that back pay."

"Nice? You wouldn't think so if you were in my shoes. They voted to have it here. And without even asking me, mind you. Some woman just said, 'I vote for having it at the

40

parsonage, the dining room's so nice and big.' And the rest all agreed and that was it."

Papa began to look worried again. "Hon, they didn't mean anything. After all, this is church property——"

"It's supposed to be our home, I thought," Mamma snapped. "They might at least have asked if it suited me. And Saturday night, of all times. Jim, have you any idea how hard it is to get my work done on Saturdays, and Sunday dinner fixed, without adding a pie supper? And Sunday morning there'll be enough to do to get the children off to Sunday school without all the extra cleaning there'll be——"

"Easter, please don't worry," Papa pleaded. "The Lord will help and so will all of us."

We all helped, even Papa, who was so big and awkward that he always just got in the way when it came to doing anything in the house. But that day he did all the boys' chores, leaving them free to help Mamma and me. It was a grueling day, but by six o'clock that evening the family had been fed, the kitchen cleaned, and the little girls bathed and dressed. Mamma announced firmly that none of us had better get any pie on our clothes, for if we did we'd take it right along to church the next day because there just weren't any changes to be had.

By seven o'clock the long dining-room table was loaded with pies of every description. Big pots of coffee, steaming on the kitchen range, filled the house with a pleasant aroma.

Completely mystified as to why Mamma hadn't liked the idea of a pie supper to raise money to give Papa, I watched in fascination as each woman cut the pie she had brought and began begging the men present to sample her wares. A piece of pie, I found, cost a dime, coffee included. Children were charged a nickel. While I was wondering how I could manage to get a piece, Mrs. Olsen, the school superintendent's wife, who was helping Mamma wash dishes in the kitchen, motioned me in there. "Get your brothers and sisters," she whispered. "I brought my pie in here. Nobody will ever miss it."

It was lemon meringue and luscious-looking. I could have spanked Dutch when she picked up her piece and announced that she preferred coconut. While I went to get a clean dish towel to tie about Pugsy's neck, since Mamma had made me responsible for seeing that she kept her dress clean, I heard Dutch saying in a shrill voice in the next room, "I'll swap you for coconut." It didn't sound so funny to me, but everybody laughed. Then a man said, "If you can eat both pieces, little girl, I'll buy you another."

Knowing I would be held responsible for Dutch also, my first instinct was to see how much pie she was getting. But just then I discovered my own untouched piece was missing. In my outrage I forgot Dutch and headed straight for the boys' room, where Rusty had retreated with his piece. He denied my charges vigorously, but because he looked entirely too satisfied to have had only one piece of pie I didn't believe him. To play safe, I gave his shin a sharp kick and ran for the safety of the kitchen with him in hot pursuit.

The kitchen was temporarily deserted, so there was nothing to do but duck into the crowded dining room, which I was sure would afford safety. But I had underestimated Rusty's wrath, or else his eyes were too crossed to notice the audience he had, for he grabbed my hair from behind and held me while he administered two sharp blows across my back.

Women squealed and men laughed, but Papa, who had witnessed the attack, did not see any humor in it. "Stop that," he yelled in a voice that outdid his best pulpit one. "Both of you go this minute into my study."

He was right behind us, and the moment the door was

closed he turned to Rusty. "What's the meaning of this, Rusty? What in the world made you forget all your upbringing and jump on your sister in public like that?"

When Rusty didn't reply, Papa showed signs of fresh outrage. "Answer me," he ordered. "What can I tell God about you this time?"

"Tell Him we were just playing," I said quickly. "Honest, that was all, Papa. Rusty wasn't mad and he didn't hurt me a bit."

Papa looked sharply at Rusty, and sure enough, my brother's hazel eyes stared straight back at him. That was evidence enough for Papa. He said, visibly relieved, "All right, I won't report you to God this time, then. But don't ever let it happen again."

The instant he'd gone I renewed the battle, knowing the strategy of a surprise attack. But two bruised shins later I fled back to the kitchen in ignominious retreat. Pugsy was there, a motley smear of pie from head to foot. Chocolate, blackberry, apple—she bore samples of all after having cleaned up the waiting dishes by way of the thumb-to-mouth method.

By ten o'clock the pie was all gone and so were the people. Only Mamma's wrath remained when she saw Pugsy, and also the dining-room floor. "Just look," she commanded Papa, sounding as though he alone were to blame. "There's pie all over the furniture and ground into the floor, the kitchen's still full of dirty dishes though I've washed for hours, and look at Pug's clothes. I'll have to wash and iron her a dress before she can go to Sunday school in the morning."

No one bothered to look at Pug, for Dutch suddenly demanded all our attention by being violently sick all over the floor. While Mamma rushed about helping her, she transferred her wrath from Papa to me.

"Ennen, how much pie did this child eat, anyway? And

where were you that you let Pug lick all the plates and Dutch eat half the pie in the house? I told you to watch them, didn't I?"

Papa answered for me. "I can tell you that, Easter. She and Rusty were playing games, chasing each other all over the house."

Before I could think of a defense plea that wouldn't annul the fib I'd told Papa, Mamma fixed me with her baleful blue eyes. "So you were playing with Rusty. Well, just bring the shovel and have fun cleaning up this floor. Then you can have the fun of doing up all those dishes while I help poor little Dutch."

While I was meditating darkly on the injustice of a world where some got pie and others got only the job of cleaning up after the rest, Rusty came into the kitchen and picked up a dish towel. "I'll wipe," he said magnanimously. When I darted him a suspicious glance he added hastily, "But I didn't take your old pie. Cross my heart."

When Rusty bothered to cross his heart, I believed him. Only then did I realize the significance of a man's voice saying to Dutch, "If you can eat both those pieces . . ." I knew then, and my heart hardened. "I hope she dies," I said bitterly. "I just hope she dies before morning."

Above the clatter of dishes as Rusty slammed them down on the table sounded Mamma's fretful voice in the next room. "Ten o'clock and half a day's work to do before I can go to bed and a sick child besides. But those women still think *they* paid you eight dollars on your back salary."

With a stack of pie plates still to wash and a hollow emptiness in my midriff, I was ready to agree with Mamma that there should be better ways of finding money to pay the preacher than giving pie suppers at the parsonage.

Truly, the parsonage belonged to the church, and the members never let us forget it. The very next afternoon, when Mamma, worn out with her night's activity and her vigil beside Dutch, tried to take the luxury of a daytime rest, a half-dozen people arrived. Two church members had brought some friends to see the parsonage. And they saw it, from the parlor, always kept ready for visitors, to the little off-porch room stacked almost to the ceiling with dirty clothes. Mamma stood quietly by while they opened closet and pantry doors, but when she saw one looking askance at the speckled dining-room floor that she hadn't yet had time to scrub, she had all she could take.

"That's pie on the floor," she said acidly. "I'm waiting for the Ladies' Aid to vote to hold something else here, then they can scrub the floor themselves."

Of course that had its repercussions. Only the next afternoon Dutch and I got home from school to find Pugsy in the kitchen just finishing a jar of jam, with Mamma nowhere in sight. The parlor door was closed, and Papa's rumbling voice led us in that direction. Dutch barged right in, leaving the door open a crack, but experience had taught me more caution. A minister's callers do not always welcome the listening ears of an almost-eleven, though they might not notice a barely-six.

Yet I lingered, filled with curiosity because of Mamma's presence and grateful for the crack Dutch had left in the door. As was to be expected, Papa was saying they should talk things over with God, but Mamma interrupted him, her voice heavy with weariness.

"I don't see any point in talking about it at all. Anybody should know I wasn't asking to have *my* floors scrubbed. It's their floor, you've all made plain to me, and it was their pie. That's all I said and all I meant."

Papa spoke again, and I recognized his trouble-ahead voice. "Sisters, I know this is all just a misunderstanding. Let us pray about it——"

Again he was interrupted, this time by a peal of laughter so sudden it was startling. Then a voice I recognized as the nice, warm one of Mrs. Olsen said, "Oh, Brother Reaves, and all of you, I think this is really funny. We *did* go off and leave pie all over the house, so why shouldn't Sister Reaves explain why her floor looked so messy? If she hadn't, those women would have gone away saying what an awful housekeeper she was. I think the next time we have something at the parsonage we ought to send in a committee to clean up afterwards."

There was a brief silence after this long speech, then Mamma's voice, so meek I scarcely recognized it: "Just vote to have something less messy than pie and I'll gladly do my own cleaning, Sister Olsen."

This brought more laughter from Mrs. Olsen, and directly the others joined in so that the parlor rang with merriment. Then Mamma had raised her voice again: "Sisters, I've just remembered I made a peach pie today. If you'll all wait a minute, I'll cut it."

There went our dessert for supper. But after I had helped Mamma carry in the plates and listened to the four women praise the pie, I didn't mind so much, for both Mamma and Papa looked relieved and happy.

After the women had left Papa put his arm about Mamma and said gently, "Easter, God knows your heart is right and so do I. Others condemn you by your words. Remember that and you can be a big help to me."

Mamma's voice shook a little as she answered, "I'll try, Jim. I really will."

6

It was early in December that I came home from school one Friday afternoon to find the big wooden barrel sitting on the front porch. I knew at once what it was, for Mamma had read aloud the letter from the Ladies' Aid of a church in Philadelphia saying they had selected us to receive their next missionary barrel and would Mamma please send sizes and ages of the family.

Nothing more than curiosity had stirred me then to ask, "What's in a missionary barrel?"

"Old clothes," Mamma said, with no enthusiasm whatever. "Things that aren't good enough for city folks to wear any more, so they send them to the missionaries' families and get themselves new."

After that I lived in dread of the arrival of that barrel, picturing the things we'd probably get and have to wear. No matter how they looked, I thought, Mamma would make us wear them. Who ever saw her let anything go to waste?

Now here was the barrel, sitting out there for all the town to see and know about our shame. Wearing old, badly worn garments was hard enough to do when they were your own things, but if it was known by everyone that the old things were a charitable donation, it just seemed to me more than I could take.

Fortunately Rusty came along, and I enlisted his sympathy and help in getting the barrel inside. Then I lived in an agony of fear that company would come in before it was opened and its contents disposed of, for Mamma insisted we must wait until after supper, when Papa would open it.

In spite of our misgivings, excitement filled us as we hurried through the dishes after supper, then gathered in the bedroom to watch the unpacking of the charity barrel.

With his claw hammer in his hand, Papa turned to Mamma. He was almost as excited as Dutch who was dancing about as though it were Christmas. "Easter, do you think it's possible they might have sent me a suit? I do need one."

I heard Mamma catch her breath as though something hurt. "Open it and see, Jim. But you know if there is a suit it won't be new. Nothing is ever new in a missionary barrel."

Papa wrenched off the head, then began lifting things from the barrel. First, a fine cashmere dress, at least two sizes too big for Mamma and obviously years behind in styling, even to our inexperienced eyes; then two old corsets someone had donated without bothering to remove the traces of wear; several pairs of women's shoes, some with exaggerated heels and pointed toes and all either too large or too small for Mamma. Nevertheless, nothing else would do Papa but that he stop while she tried them on, Dutch and Pugsy helping. The large pair had the highest heels, and we all shrieked with laughter as she teetered across the room, tripping over her own feet.

Next Papa pulled out some long underwear and held it up. "Well, well, this must be for me." Then we all screamed with laughter again, for Papa was over six feet tall and the underclothes must have once belonged to a runt. Mamma took them and looked them over critically. "I can fix them for Rusty," she decided.

More underwear, woolen. Doubtless it had belonged to a large man like Papa, but it had been shrunk in washing until it looked hopeless. But Mamma said staunchly, "They're still good. I can wet and stretch them."

Underpants for Mamma, the kind with open flaps behind. Mamma snatched them out of Papa's hands before the boys could get a good look. "Well, thank goodness, I get something," she said.

Hats, hats, hats. Crushed felts, straws with faded bunches of flowers, a hard derby that perched ridiculously on the top of Papa's head. I asked, puzzled, "Why do they send all those old hats?"

Mamma's reply was just as confusing: "So they can buy new ones with a clear conscience."

More shoes, these for men. Red seized a pair and with an effort got his big feet inside them. "I can wear them, Mamma. They're just a little small."

"You'll do no such thing," Mamma said firmly. "Nobody's going to send you more feet when yours are ruined."

Papa had to stoop now to lift out garments. He straightened up, clutching a mass of dark wool in his hands. "Easter, I do believe it's a suit. Did you send them my size when they wrote us?"

"Of course," Mamma said. "I sent all the sizes, but they must not have looked at the letter. For pity's sake, hold it up and let's see, Jim."

Papa held it up, and this time there was no laughter. Only a stunned silence. The suit was the kind we had seen pictured for ballroom wear—long, flapping tails, a cutaway front, satin-striped trousers. And obviously too small for Papa.

Mamma broke the silence, her voice having an odd, hollow

49

sound. "A dancing suit for a preacher. They must have got that in by mistake."

A few more articles that didn't appear entirely useless came out of the barrel, including a pair of trousers badly needed by Red. Then Papa held up a girl's coat. Are the thrills of such rare moments ever forgotten? It looked like my size, yet I dared not hope. It looked brand-new, but I dared not believe it could be. In fact, I scarcely dared breathe as Papa turned it about to examine it from every angle. "It looks new, Easter." His voice was filled with awe. "And I do believe it's just Ennen's size."

I knew then, and I was completely overcome with awe. I sat glued to my chair, trembling all over, terribly afraid I'd burst out crying. That coat, I knew, had not come from any benevolent group of women making a charitable gesture. It was a gift from God, a direct answer to the nightly prayer I'd been secretly saying for weeks—ever since I had asked Papa if I might possibly get a new coat and he had said, as he always said to every request, "We'll have to pray about it, Ennen."

So I had prayed, though without much hope of getting the answer I wanted so terribly. I'd never owned a coat. In Waco I had worn Mamma's light serge cape to school on bad days. It had already proved to be inadequate for this colder climate, and it was badly worn. I wanted a brand-new coat more than I'd ever wanted anything in my life, and here it was, silk lining, velvet buttons, and all.

Mamma was saying, with a happy lilt in her voice, "Try it on, Ennen. Oh my, I do hope it fits."

It fitted perfectly. It was gorgeously beautiful, it was a miracle of miracles coming out of that barrel of useless old things.

Then Mamma almost spoiled it. Her happy glow faded, and worry lines appeared in her face as she fingered the soft fabric.

"I don't understand, Jim. It's an awfully good coat and brand-new. Do you suppose it could have got in by mistake?"

"Oh, no, no!" I clutched the coat tighter about me, unable to make my protest more than a terrified whisper. "It's mine, Mamma. I know it is."

I wanted to tell her I'd prayed for it, but I was too self-conscious. The boys would be sure to laugh. Even Mamma herself might laugh. I wasn't at all sure how Mamma felt about miracles. I wasn't even sure how Papa felt. He always said, "Let us pray about it," or "The Lord will provide," but sometimes he looked very worried as he said it, and sometimes he prayed so long I had the feeling he was trying to talk God into being on his side. But now I knew that prayer could bring results, and I knew I'd just die if Mamma didn't let me keep that lovely coat.

All day Saturday I suffered, slipping into the bedroom every once in a while just to look at the coat and offer a quick prayer for snow, ice, or bitter winds—anything to make Mamma soften and tell me to wear the coat to church for my health's sake.

Again my prayers seemed answered. Early Sunday morning a cold wind blew up. Mamma looked out at the gray skies and sighed, "It's going to be a real norther, Ennen. I'm going to let you wear that coat to church. If somebody made a mistake it was theirs, not ours."

That morning I really hurried with the dishes and with Dutch's hair, which I had to braid every morning, and Pugsy's curls, which ordinarily I liked to linger over. Both got what Mamma called a lick and a promise—just a hasty brushing over tangles it took too long to comb out. Then I rushed them to the church, to be sure I was there in all my regal splendor to impress Trudy when she arrived wearing the new coat about which she had been bragging.

51

"Papa bought it at Freeman's store," she had told me again and again. "He paid twelve dollars for it. Why doesn't your folks buy you a new coat?"

"They're going to pretty soon." The lie had just voiced itself and had lain heavily on my conscience ever since, adding fervency to my prayers for a coat. Now I felt purged, exonerated! Now Trudy would see I hadn't been just talking. Already I had forgotten that intent makes the lie.

Because her coat was still new, Trudy was also early. She looked satisfactorily impressed at sight of me, as did her mother. Mrs. Wilson had me stand up so she could examine the fit and look at the lining and make sure it really was new. Then she said acidly, "Well, it's pretty, all right, but it seems to me a cheaper coat would have done for folks so hard up. Where did you buy it, Ennen?"

Then everything was spoiled as I visualized that awful barrel of old clothes, sick at what I had to admit. Did I have to tell about that? Did I have to?

Trudy and her mother, I thought, were watching me closely, ready to pounce and denounce me before the world. As though already tasting her triumph, Trudy preened herself a little and repeated what she'd already said numberless times: "We bought mine at Freeman's and paid twelve dollars for it. Did you buy yours there? How much did it cost?"

Never shall I long to do anything as I longed to say that day that my lovely coat had also come from Freeman's. That would have made me feel a normal person in a normal world, living and acting as did others around me, instead of being set apart and different because Papa was a preacher. But this time I could not compromise with the truth. Reason forbade it. Anyone would know that a coat like mine had never hung on a rack in Freeman's, and if they doubted they could soon make

52

sure. But Trudy and her mother were waiting, and I had to make some explanation.

Then, as happened all too often, imagination came to my rescue. Suddenly I was hearing Papa ask one of our overnight guests what he sold on the road and his answer was, "Women's and children's wearing apparel." In a flash of what I felt then was direct inspiration, I heard myself saying, "Papa bought mine from a drummer that stayed with us but I don't know what it cost."

From the envy in Trudy's eyes I knew I had scored a hit. My triumph was sweet, though short-lived. During Sunday school it boomeranged.

Because of the absence of the regular teacher, Mr. Olsen taught the girls that morning, including Trudy and me. He was a kindly man, an educator by choice because he wanted to help young people prepare themselves for a good life. Yet he unknowingly crucified me that morning as he talked about the value of doing kind deeds and for some reason illustrated his point by mentioning the missionary barrel the pastor's family had just received from perfect strangers. I saw Trudy dart a suspicious glance at me, and I froze inside as I waited for what I knew in my guilty heart was coming. And it came, accompanied by a kindly twinkle in Mr. Olsen's eyes.

"I see they put in a very pretty coat for Ennen, too."

It was bitterly humiliating. With a choked cry I jumped up and rushed out of the door and toward the refuge of home. Mamma was just coming across the yard, late as usual, and stopped to ask what in the world was the matter. Sobbing "Nothing," I rushed past her, but she turned around and followed me into the house. There she got the whole story from me, even the fib about the drummer.

To my surprise she didn't scold, but her voice was the grim

one I always dreaded to hear as she stood up. "You come on back to church." she said sternly. "You're not going to let Trudy Wilson crow over you."

Washing the tears off my face, I went back with Mamma, my head high but my heart thudding painfully. Mamma led me straight to Professor Olsen, just about ready to dismiss his group. "Brother Olsen," she said, in a voice none of the girls could fail to hear, "you almost spoiled Ennen's Christmas coat, saying it came out of that missionary barrel. I think you ought to tell her friends you were just guessing about that and that you never saw one of those barrels or you'd know there is never anything new in them."

It was a masterpiece of evasion that held me spellbound with admiration. I felt like kneeling in homage to Mamma, for with all my practice I knew I could never have done so well. Professor Olsen's apology was sweet music in my ears, still ringing when we went home after church.

The music stopped abruptly the instant I saw Papa's face. The good Professor, it seemed, had also apologized to Papa, and the news of Mamma's conspiracy with me to deceive had not brought joy to his heart. But because he was wary about reproving Mamma, he came directly to me for an explanation as to why I had lied about getting the coat from the missionary barrel. Before I could think of an answer Mamma came to my rescue.

"Because she's got some pride, Jim. And I mean to see that she keeps it. So no need to say any more about it."

Papa stared at her in utter unbelief. "But pride like that is wrong, Easter. Just like it's wrong to lie——"

"It's also wrong to kill a child's spirit by making her feel like a pauper," Mamma retorted. "Jim, she's going to learn soon enough that pride like hers goes before a fall. Just let her alone

54

to learn in her own way or I'll start telling folks in this town a few things."

A threat like that from Mamma was not to be ignored. Papa dropped the subject; but the next night at family altar time he prayed a long time for forgiveness of sins, pointing out to God what a sinful thing pride was and how unworthy every sinful soul was to receive His blessings.

By the time he finished I felt seared with guilt, and I wondered how I could ever set myself right with God so I might dare pray for other things I wanted. After that some of my pleasure in my lovely new coat was gone. I could never put it on without a return of that intense feeling of guilt.

Mamma was very wise.

7

Our first Christmas in the parsonage was a memorable one. In our quiet private life in Texas we had made Christmas a time of joy in sharing: the joyous ceremony of hanging stockings on Christmas Eve, excited speculation about what we might expect, a simple feast, and the singing of carols gathered about Mamma at the wheezy reed organ—truly a time of peace and good will among ourselves.

Suddenly all that was changed. Our Christmas Eve fun had to be shared with all at the church program around the big tree. That would have been all right, though, if the little devils of envy had not reared their ugly heads, when the other girls my age began bragging about what they would get off the tree. It was, we learned, the practice of the church members to bring the choicest gift they had for their child and hang it on the church tree to be presented publicly. In addition to these family presents, each child present received a small bag of hard candy from the church.

At first I couldn't understand how the girls knew what to expect off the tree. The element of complete surprise was an important part of our Christmas, but not apparently with these new friends. Their parents discussed Christmas gifts as they might a family outing, and they were permitted to select what they wanted.

But Mamma didn't see it like that. When I asked her what we would get off the church tree, she had her answer ready. "Nothing. What you kids get you'll get at home like you always do. Why take it to church to make a show about it?"

"Well, the others all get something," I argued. "Trudy's going to get a big doll that goes to sleep and Freda Barret wants a sled and Freda's little sister will get a doll buggy——"

Mamma said tersely, and I had no way of knowing how the words must have hurt her, "You kids won't get much this year. That doesn't mean we can't have a happy Christmas if we all do our part. But expensive presents are out. And what you do get, you'll get in your stocking as always."

Though barely eleven then, I was old enough to understand how changed was our economic situation. In Texas we hadn't been wholly financially dependent upon Papa's small pay as a minister, for Mamma, with the boys' help, had kept several cows and sold milk and butter. At times she had boarders, and always there had been a small but steady income from her chickens. Now the family used all the milk produced by the two cows, and the flock of chickens had been reduced in number until we seldom had all the eggs we needed. And the boarders stayed for free because we lived in a church parsonage.

So the outlook for Christmas was gloomy at best, and I divided my sympathies between my sisters, too young to understand, and myself. But it was a busy season, with program rehearsals every afternoon, and in spite of my dread of finding us all left out when the gifts were distributed at the church, Christmas Eve was suddenly there and I hadn't found a way to prepare Dutch and Pug for what I feared would be a terrible disappointment.

57

Right after breakfast Papa and Red nailed a base to the big cedar and carried it into the church. Then the decorating committee of women arrived and went to work. By noon they were gone and the church was locked again, but with Rusty's help and some boxes stacked under the window Dutch and I were able to climb up and peer in.

It was a beautiful tree, so large the topmost star almost touched the ceiling. The limbs sparkled with tufts of white cotton and strings of popcorn and cranberries, and hanging from the tips of the bending limbs were luscious-looking popcorn balls. With my nose flattened against the cold glass, I stared and stared but saw no signs of presents for anyone. Greatly relieved, I climbed down to let Dutch take my place. It didn't really matter that we would receive nothing if only the others didn't get presents.

After the noon dishes were done, Mamma, no doubt worrying about the same thing I was, surprised us by giving each of us fifteen cents, telling us that we might go to town and buy something we wanted.

"Mind you, each one gets to pick what she wants. Ennen, you help Pugsy, and Rusty can help Dutch. I don't hold with this sort of thing, but if everybody else gets something I guess you can too."

It was truly exciting to be allowed to pick your own gift, and I knew what I would choose. A book. When you bought a book you bought a whole new world, to live in through out the year. Yes, I decided, a book would look good on the tree. Not as impressive as a doll that shut its eyes and had real hair, but an exciting new book was not to be scorned.

It took a long time for Dutch and Pugsy to decide what they wanted. After Pugsy had appropriated a toy she refused to give up her precious coins to pay for it, and it took the combined efforts of all of us, with the help of the sales clerk and the store manager, to take them away from her. Dutch changed her mind half a dozen times, but after I had delivered an ultimatum she decided she would keep the glittering strand of shiny glass beads, which I knew in my heart would not please Mamma. But they pleased Dutch, so I was helpless.

At last I was free to revel in a row of books and had just about made my decision when Rusty came up, his eyes shining. "Hey, Skinny, come over here. I got something to show you."

The "something" was an exquisite little china high hat, decorated with rosebuds and resting on its top. I stared at it stupidly. "What is it, Rusty?"

"A toothpick holder, stupid. Ain't it just about the slickest thing you ever saw?"

I'd never heard such awe in Rusty's voice, and I couldn't believe my ears. Rusty choosing a toothpick holder? That, instead of a knife or baseball or top or marbles? "Are you really gonna buy it, Rusty?"

"I will if you will. It'll take all our money. See? It's marked thirty cents."

"No," I said, clutching my precious money tighter. "I'm going to get a book. I don't want a toothpick holder."

"Neither do I, stupid. It's for Mamma. Gee whiz, somebody ought to buy her something, hadn't they?"

My jaw went slack, my body cold. I'd never once thought about who would provide a Christmas present for Mamma. But Rusty, the black sheep, had. Shame flooded me as I thrust my money into his hand. "Here, you buy it."

We were a happy group as we trudged home. True, Dutch broke the string of her beads before we got there, and all she had was a fistful of glass baubles and a tear-streaked face. And Pugsy had dropped her toy and then stepped on it, so that it hardly looked presentable to hang on the tree. But Rusty proudly and carefully carried the box in which reposed the dainty china hat, and the true spirit of Christmas flooded my heart so that it was singing without my quite knowing why.

Then came the excitement of trying to smuggle the box into the house without Mamma seeing it, of finding a safe hiding place until morning. With much giggling and whispering we secreted it in Rusty's Sunday shoe, then every little while one of us would think of a better place and we'd go through it all again. After much debating we decided against taking it to the church. It was so fragile it might get broken. Besides, Mamma would not want to receive something off the tree when none of the rest of us did.

It required considerable tact and diplomacy to parry her questions as to what we got for ourselves, and long before time to start for the church I had decided it was lots more fun to buy something for someone else than for yourself. Yet as we entered the church and I saw how the cedar tree had blossomed with gifts since noon, I had a queasy feeling in the pit of my stomach. All the things the girls had said they would receive were there, plus many more. It looked like gifts enough for every child in town, and I had to shut my eyes tight and visualize Mamma's face when she saw that beautiful toothpick holder before the small pangs of envy would go away.

The program, which we had practiced untiringly, went off very well, even if Dutch did forget the Bible verse she was to say, in which I had drilled her endlessly. With her usual poise she calmly substituted a nursery rhyme that brought a few titters over the house, but no one tried to stop her. Poor Rusty, who had protested bitterly over his role as one of the Wise Men, tripped over his robe and fell flat on his stomach, but he got up so fast there was no real interruption. I was Mary, with nothing to do but sit beside the cradle in which Pugsy lay and make threats under my breath every time she moved.

Trudy had coveted that role, but all agreed that Pugsy might lie still for me but she surely wouldn't for Trudy.

At last the "exercises" were over and we were all back in our seats, facing that exciting tree. There was a commotion at the door, and we turned to see Santa Claus coming down the aisle, complete with white whiskers and hair, red suit, big stomach, and bulging pack over his shoulder.

From the pack he handed each child a red bag of candy and nuts, making jocular remarks as he did so. When that was done he turned to the tree and, rubbing his hands together, said in his best Santa Claus voice, "Well, well, I see my helper has left some more things here for good little boys and girls. I guess I'd better see that they go to the right places."

Then he began lifting off objects and calling out names, to the accompaniment of squeals of excitement as each child called ran forward to receive his or her gift. I clenched my hands and controlled my pangs of jealousy, as did Dutch. But not Pugsy. As the last present was taken down, the big doll for Trudy, Pugsy let out a screech that seemed to shake the rafters. "I want a doll too! Santa Claus, give me a doll like hers."

Mamma reached her and smothered her cries, and Papa's voice boomed out a benediction. Then, with excited children still swarming about Santa Claus, Mamma marched up to him, leading the sobbing Pugsy by the hand and trailed by a solemn-eyed Dutch.

"Brother Bullock," Mamma said, her voice ringing loud and clear over the hubbub of talk and laughter, "I want you to take off that mask and show her you're not really Santa Claus."

Silence fell over the room as every head turned to stare at Mamma and the rattled Santa, who attempted to bluster it out. "Why, Sister Reaves, of course I'm Santa——"

"You're not," Mamma said flatly, "and I want these children

61

who didn't get anything off that tree, and there's more here than mine who didn't, to know you're just playing a game. Either you show them or I will."

Brother Bullock, known to all of us, took off his mask, grinning sheepishly. "Well, now, I guess we were just having fun, wasn't we, Sister Reaves?"

Mamma's lips were tight, her voice hard. "That's right. Only it wasn't any fun for some of the children."

There were whispers behind us as we walked toward the door, but I felt strangely happy. It helped to say to Trudy, clutching her big doll against her, as we went past, "It's a pretty doll but I thought you were too big for dolls, Trudy. I certainly am."

Right then I felt very big and grown up, for I didn't envy a soul in all the world.

That was the last Christmas at our church when the church members brought gifts for their own children. By unanimous vote the next year it was agreed to have only the program and the treats, share and share alike.

Any disappointment of the little girls was forgotten the next morning when they took down their stockings. I don't know how she managed, but Mamma had provided small gifts to delight their hearts. There was a book for me, and a pair of stockings and some candy.

But it wouldn't have mattered if I hadn't gotten anything after I saw Mamma's face when Rusty nonchalantly dropped the little box into her lap. While she opened it, her hands shaking a little, I explained how we had managed to get it, wanting to be sure I got my share of the credit.

The light that filled Mamma's face as she lifted out the small china object was something to remember. "It's simply beautiful," she said, so ardently that I began to wonder if I'd been lacking in art appreciation. "It's exactly what I've always wanted."

From that day on no table was ever set by my mother that the small container, filled with toothpicks, didn't grace the middle, a silent reminder that it really is more fun to give than to receive.

8

The poet who writes so feelingly of the house by the side of the road never lived in a frontier parsonage. Ours was, literally, a haven for all travelers through that part of the Indian Territory, weary or otherwise.

Because our small town was on the railroad and surrounded by rich farm land, it attracted many legitimate traveling salesmen, many bogus ones, and many men looking for opportunities of one kind or another. Even some just looking for adventure.

Because of the meager hotel facilities the town afforded, finding a place to sleep often presented a real problem to the traveling public. Or it did until the new Baptist parsonage was built and turned over to Parson Reaves as a temporary home. The parsonage promptly became the traveler's answer to prayer. Soon the word spread throughout the Territory that all a stranded man had to do was look up the parson and tell his hard-luck story. It helped, they found out, to expand on how stanch a Christian they or their fathers or grandfathers were, though Papa did not demand his own brand of faith. Once Mamma asked Papa if it did not seem strange to him that all the traveling men had minister fathers, but Papa only replied smilingly that preachers were noted for their large families.

Word of Papa's gullibility, as Mamma frankly called it, must have spread on the winds that first winter, because it quickly became a rare night that some stranger didn't sleep under the parsonage roof. And who was Mamma to object? After all, she had daily reminders that the house didn't belong to her. And if she complained, Papa just looked grieved and replied that he was a servant of God and the men to whom they gave shelter were strangers within their gates, maybe even angels unaware. What answer could she make to that? Secretly I thought she might have tried harder to find one if Papa hadn't so obviously enjoyed the stream of guests.

Within a month after our moving into the parsonage, a bed was put up in Papa's study and it became a sort of assembly-line guest room for travelers. Sometimes one stranger was settling down even as another was leaving, and quite often strangers gratefully shared the bed. Sheets, however, were changed only once a week, as they were on the other beds, unless some guest left too evident a reminder of his occupancy.

Besides the extra work for Mamma, this continuous program of entertaining created serious money difficulties. Papa never took his hospitality duties lightly. When he invited a man into his home, the invitation included meals when they were needed—most certainly breakfast, often supper. And Papa's meager salary hardly provided for so many.

Though he had been called as a full-time pastor, the church agreed to pay Papa only thirty dollars a month, and often this was in arrears for several months at a time. But no matter how poor the collections on Sunday became, Papa would not have desecrated his pulpit by even the mention of pay for his work. He labored for God and gratefully took what was offered him, asking nothing more than the people wanted to give. If

Mamma sometimes thought he ought to stir them up into wanting to give, who can blame her? But Papa's answer was always the same: "It wouldn't be a love offering if I made them feel they had to give, Easter. That way I'd be cheating them."

To supplement the small salary offered by the church, the Baptist Home Mission Board added twenty dollars a month. Any territorial church, except in the larger places, was considered a mission post.

This twenty dollars from the Board could be relied upon and often had to be stretched to meet all the household needs. But Mamma was adept at stretching. Fortunately, two prominent church members owned grocery stores, and as a matter of policy Papa tried to trade with both. So Mamma arranged to rotate her business, this month buying from Brother Rodman, the next Brother Cragmore. That way she could count on a month's extra leeway; for if there wasn't enough to meet Brother Rodman's bill at the end of the month, she could hope there would be by the time his turn arrived again, when Brother Cragmore would have to wait. I think Mamma secretly hoped they would complain sometimes, so that she could enter a counter complaint!

Doubtless Mamma didn't worry nearly as much as I thought she did. She'd sit at the table, her blue eyes snapping and her voice grim: "Better enjoy this food, everybody. It's the last in the house and I don't know where any more is coming from." But the next day would be a repetition of the day before. Perhaps Mamma only worried aloud so much because Papa never seemed to worry at all. His stock answer to every anxiety voiced by Mamma was, "The Lord will provide, honey. Let's just trust in Him."

We kids weren't certain whether his trust was more in Mamma or the Lord, but we definitely leaned toward Mamma.

Papa trusted men almost as completely as he trusted God.

Everyone who came along was accepted on faith, often with embarrassing results that Mamma never let him forget—such as the time he accompanied his current house guest, an Easterner with an impressive gift of diction who called himself Professor, on a house-to-house campaign collecting money for a nonexistent home for homeless children. Papa and the town might never have known he was the victim of a confidence man if the self-termed professor hadn't had an hour or so to wait for his train and met up with a man who had a Texas bottle he offered to share. The result was that the professor missed his train. He then confided to his drinking companion that he was reluctant to go back to the parsonage with liquor on his breath, possibly embarrassing the good parson after he'd been kind enough to help him swindle his members and the townspeople out of twenty-five dollars.

Mamma made the most of that, reminding Papa that he should have been collecting money to feed his own children. But Papa was ready to sympathize with and help the next man who came in the name of a worthy cause or with a hard-luck story.

Not all visitors at the parsonage were dead beats, however. Many a grateful legitimate salesman left half a dollar on the bed to insure his next welcome. And there were many "regulars" who demonstrated their appreciation of the parsonage hospitality in whatever way they could.

Among these was an apple peddler who came periodically from across the Canadian River in Oklahoma Territory, bringing a wagonload of apples which he sold from door to door.

Always "Apple" Benson was welcomed by saint and sinners alike. Whether he stayed at the parsonage for one night or longer, he gave Mamma a bushel of apples for each night, not to mention all we consumed from his wagon, for he never reproved us for climbing over the wheels to help ourselves.

When Mamma scolded us about it he'd shake his head, his long white whiskers waving gently like peace banners. "Don't you bother your head about that, Sister Reaves. They're God's apples and God's younguns. Why shouldn't they get together?"

Apple Benson was a devout man of another faith than ours. If he spent a week end with us he gave Rusty a quarter to help him on Saturday, and it was from my brother that we learned about the old man's sales technique.

Together they'd lug a basket of apples to a door, and when the woman of the house answered his knock the old man would greet her by name and would add, "You need some of God's apples today?" And after every sale the ritual was the same. Apple Benson dropped to his bony knees, face raised to the sky and whiskers wagging as though in salute, to thank God for letting him deliver some of His apples into that home. A bushel of red, juicy apples for twenty-five cents with a prayer thrown in. Not many women could offer sales resistance to Apple Benson.

For weeks after a visit from Apple Benson we'd eat apples, raw, stewed, baked, or fried. No one has ever yet offered me a delicacy to match Mamma's baked apple dumplings. If the study bed happened to be occupied when Apple Benson arrived, one of the boys gladly took the floor to give him his place in bed.

Another peddler who took pride in paying for his board with his product was a self-styled physician who came periodically every winter for several years, selling his own guaranteed remedy for catarrh. The doctor, however, failed to meet with the welcome we gave the apple peddler. His visits meant extra laundry work for Mamma, for he was so untidy she wouldn't permit a subsequent guest to use the same bed linens. His person, she was sure, was as much in need of washing as his clothes.

68

The first time Doctor White sat down at our table I saw Mamma look at his grimy, dirt-encrusted hands in dismay. Then she proceeded to inspect each of ours, sending both Rusty and me away from the table suffering acute humiliation. "Go wash up before you set at my table," she said firmly. How could we understand that she was talking over our heads to her self-invited guest?

Apparently he never knew it, either. He continued to come regularly, often staying several days at a time. Mamma continued to threaten to tell him he had to bathe or leave, but she never did. And for every night's stay in the parsonage Doctor White left a bottle of White's Famous Catarrh Cure. What did it matter that none of us had catarrh? He did what he could, as Papa pointed out. In time she accepted the self-styled doctor, his untidiness and his cure-all, carefully putting each bottle received on the pantry shelf. Years later the collection had assumed such proportions that I begged Mamma to let me throw them away, but she refused indignantly. "Indeed you won't. I earned that stuff and I'm keeping it, though goodness knows I wouldn't take it if I was dying."

One time, I remember, Mamma openly rebelled. Papa brought in a man and a youth who looked as though they'd never slept in a bed or used a washbasin. "These are Brother Case's kin," he told Mamma. "His wife isn't feeling well, and he's asked us to keep them a day or so."

Brother Case was a prosperous farmer living a mile or so from town, a member of Papa's church and a fairly generous contributor. So in spite of the fact that Mamma knew this meant extra laundry, as in the case of Doctor White, she knew she had to comply with the request. But she hit on a bright idea—she thought.

The boy was about Red's age, so she told Red to invite him to share his Saturday night bath with him, hoping the father might also take the hint. She even gave Red a clean night-shirt to offer the boy and prompted him on how to suggest to the older man that he could use the little washroom after the boys had finished, if he cared to.

After his bath Red came to report to Mamma. "His clothes is full of funny flat bugs. They're crawling all over your clothes in there now. I caught one and here it is. What is it, anyway?"

Mamma shrieked at sight of his specimen, then started for Papa with fire in her eyes. "Jim, get those people out of here. Right now. They're crawling with bedbugs."

Papa tried to placate her. "I told Brother Case we'd keep them till his wife is better——"

"I don't care what you told him," Mamma declared in no uncertain tone. "I'm telling you they can't stay here another minute. Already they've likely got my house full of those nasty things. Now you send them right back to Case or I'll have to do it."

Papa was helpless when Mamma really went to battle. We never did know how he explained to his guests, but a half-hour later they drove off in Papa's buggy toward the Case farm, the youth richer by one nightshirt, as neither Red nor Mamma wanted it back.

Most of the rest of the night Mamma and Red spent shaking out the soiled garments in the washroom and killing the bugs that had found their way into them. Bedbugs, according to Mamma, were prolific little pests that must not be allowed harbor for even one night.

The next day Farmer Case brought Papa's buggy back in a very resentful frame of mind. "I can't understand why you sent my cousin and his boy back to my place last night, Brother Reaves. I had to put them in the barn because my wife had already refused to let anybody so dirty sleep in the house."

After that the bed in the study got a thorough inspection

after every visitor left. And whenever Papa returned from staying overnight with one of his country members or from spending a fifth Sunday preaching in a rural community, Mamma met him at the door, drew him quickly into the kitchen, and made him disrobe. Then every garment was inspected minutely and he was required to take a bath before he could feel he was welcome at home again.

Anything could come to the parsonage, and almost everything did. But no bedbugs got past Mamma's eagle eye.

9

When Papa read the letter aloud, my first thought was that it would be nice to have a woman guest for a change. This woman had written from Texas, saying her cousin knew someone who knew Papa and she—the cousin—had suggested writing to ask if she might stay at the parsonage during the few days' visit she planned to make in our town. She was a lone widow and timid about staying in a hotel among strangers.

Papa finished reading and looked at Mamma. "What shall I write her, Easter?"

Mamma gave him a withering look. "Why ask me? Go on and mail that letter you've already written."

Papa grinned sheepishly. "Well, honey, I knew what you would say. We couldn't let a lone woman stay at that place. And after all, she'll only be here a day or so."

But when Mrs. Martin arrived a week later she brought along a great deal of luggage for a stay of only a few days. Clyde Peterson's father, who ran the only dray in town, brought out two big trunks and two valises, completely filling the small guest room that still had Papa's desk and bookcases in it.

72

Mrs. Martin appeared to be well past thirty, and she was not unattractive for a woman of that age, for she wore very striking and expensive clothes. At least Mamma said they were expensive when she cornered Papa that night. "What did she bring all those clothes for if she's only staying a day or two? And mighty expensive clothes, if you ask me. Jim, what does she want here?"

"Easter, I couldn't ask her that. She asked a lot of questions about this country and the people, says she might decide to stay."

"Well, I hope she doesn't decide just to stay with us."

Two weeks later Mamma was saying that must be what Mrs. Martin had decided. She didn't mention leaving and seemed very satisfied. Every morning she came out of her room arrayed in a fancy costume that cost more than all Mamma's wardrobe, ate a hearty breakfast Mamma had prepared without any assistance from her, then looked archly at Papa. "Brother Reaves, may I make calls with you again this morning? I do so enjoy meeting the wonderful people and seeing the country."

Papa's calls often took him into the country for several miles, and he and Mrs. Martin might be gone all day. At night, when supper and prayer time were over and our guest had retired to Papa's study—from which he was now exiled—Mamma repeated her question.

"Jim, did she mention leaving today? Can't you tell by now what she's after?"

Papa began to sound troubled as he replied, "Easter, she just don't talk about her business. All I can say is she seems nice. I just don't know why she wants to tag around after me like that unless . . ."

Lying in bed in the next room, I held my breath waiting for Papa to finish that sentence and solve the mystery of Mrs.

Martin, but at that point he always lowered his voice. Then one night he raised instead of lowering it.

"I tell you, Easter, she's looking for a husband."

"Well, she can leave mine alone," Mamma said. "Jim, I'm going to tell her she's got to go."

"Easter, honey, we can't do that. After all, she is a widow so we've got an obligation about her. Let's give her a little more time."

The next morning on the way to school I told Red and Rusty what I'd overheard. Red said thoughtfully, "So she wants a man, eh? You know what, kids? I think we ought to help her get one so she gets out of here."

The idea appealed strongly to me, but Rusty was skeptical. "How can we help her? We don't know any unmarried men."

"There's Doctor White," Red said, grinning. "He ought to be coming back most any day."

I said with conviction, "She wouldn't have him. He's too dirty."

"She hasn't seen him, has she?" Then Red shut up, as he had a way of doing.

That night, as soon as the cows were milked and the wood brought in, Red and Rusty shut themselves up in their room. I knew something important was going on, and it was almost more than I could bear not to be in on it. If it had been just Rusty, I would have gone in and demanded a share in whatever secret he had, but I stood a little in awe of Red, four years older than I.

At the supper table that night Red asked Mamma when Doctor White would be back. Mamma looked at the calendar hanging on the wall and sighed, "Maybe in a couple of weeks." She added pointedly. "But I don't know where in the world I'll put him."

Mrs. Martin disregarded the hint. "Who is Doctor White?" Her voice was alert with interest.

Red made haste to answer. "He's a patent-medicine manufacturer. Comes through here once in a while. You ought to set your cap for him, Mrs. Martin. He's unmarried, too."

She blushed, her eyes sparkling. "Oh, my, how you do talk, Red. But there'll never be another man who can take my dear husband's place." Almost in the same breath she asked, "Has he got any money?"

Mamma answered that, innocently taking part in Red's plot. "He ought to be rich. He certainly never spends any."

Red asked nonchalantly, "Isn't this his week in Ardmore?"

Mamma gave him a sharp glance. "I think so. But why all the sudden interest in Doctor White? He's not due yet, thank goodness."

"Oh, I was just thinking he might come earlier this time. If he does, don't worry, Mamma. I'll sleep in the floor and give him my place."

"You will not, you double-crosser!" The explosion came from Rusty, whose eyes were beginning to cross. "We drew straws fair and square and I won. I get the floor and he sleeps with you."

"You cheated on those straws. They were both short and you know it."

"Here, here, boys. What's this all about?" Mamma was looking from one to the other of my brothers, frankly puzzled. "Why in the world are you arguing about something that might not even happen?" She looked again at her guest as she added, "Maybe neither of you will have to sleep with him since he's not due for a couple of weeks or more."

Red said hastily, "I just said in case he did come earlier this time. You can't tell about a man like Doctor White, rich enough to travel all over the country. He just might drop in any day."

Mamma sighed. "Well, let's hope not."

After supper Mrs. Martin offered, for the first time, to help Rusty and me with the dishes. "Tell me more about Doctor White," she said, smiling at Rusty archly. "He sounds simply fascinating. Is he handsome as well as rich? Mr. Martin, my dear departed husband, was such a handsome man."

I looked at Rusty and broke into giggles, but he kept a straight face as he answered the widow, "Gosh, I dunno. Tell you what, Mrs. Martin, I'll draw you a picture of him."

Rusty, shy with words, could always express himself in pictures that were often startlingly realistic. So while the widow polished glasses, he took a ruled tablet and a stubby pencil and after a little while held up a picture for us to see. "Here, I guess he looks sort of like that."

He did indeed. Except for the grimy clothes and dirt encrustations on his hands and neck and head that Mamma had found so offensive, it was a good likeness of Doctor White. Allowing, of course, for the rare times the doctor had not neglected to shave.

Mrs. Martin's eyes bugged with excitement as she stared down at Rusty's artistic efforts. "Oh, my! He is right handsome, isn't he? It would be nice if he came while I am here, wouldn't it? I'd surely like to meet him."

Rusty threw me an oddly triumphant glance. "I bet he does." He spoke so positively that I looked at him in surprise, intending to remind him of what Mamma had said. But he was already hurrying off to his room, apparently fearful that Mrs. Martin might lose interest in her new task of dish-drying. I had a strong feeling my brothers were plotting something, and I suffered terribly at the thought that they were excluding me from their confidence.

During the next week the doctor was a constant topic of conversation at the parsonage, whenever Mrs. Martin could get the boys' attention. Listening to Red and Rusty praise the patent-medicine vendor, I began to wonder if I had greatly misjudged the personal charm they saw in him.

Mamma and I were preparing supper one night when Rusty burst into the kitchen. "He's here," he shouted. "I saw him getting off the train. Where's Mrs. Martin?"

Mamma fixed him with her sharp eyes. "Where do you think she is? Tagging around after your papa, of course. And who's here, I'd like to know?"

"Doctor White. Red wrote him a letter to Ardmore and told him to hurry because we had a rich widow who wanted to meet him."

Mamma gave a startled gasp. "Red wrote to Doctor White? Whatever on earth for?"

"I told you. To get rid of Mrs. Martin for you. Didn't Papa say she was looking for a man?"

"Looking for a man? Oh, my goodness." Mamma broke into a peal of laughter so unexpected it was startling. "You mean that's why you two have been talking up that old man to her? Heavens above, you can't think even she wants one that bad."

"He's a man," Rusty said. There was no time to say anything more, for just then there was a sound of buggy wheels in the yard and Papa's loud "Whoa!" In a flash Rusty was through the back door, shouting his news. "He's here, Mrs. Martin. Doctor White got off the train a while ago and stopped in the drugstore to sell them some cure. He'll be here in time for supper, I bet."

There was an answering squeal of excitement from the widow as she came hurrying into the house. "Oh, my, and what a fright I must look." She ran through the kitchen in a flurry of skirts, and we heard the study door slam. Mamma

77

looked after her, her face a conflict of amusement and consternation. "Well," she said, "what Jim ought to do to those boys . . ."

Just as Papa came in, having turned his team over to Red and Rusty to unhitch and care for, the knock on the front door heralded the arrival of our second guest. Mamma said firmly, all traces of her mirth gone, "Jim, go tell him he'll have to hunt another free bed. I haven't got time nor grub for promoting any romances."

Papa gave her a troubled and puzzled glance, then dutifully answered the front door. His booming voice carried clearly to the kitchen. "Well, well, if it isn't Doctor White. Come right in, Doctor, and make yourself at home. We're just about ready to sit down to supper."

Mamma sighed. "Get out another place, Ennen. And just wait till I get my hands on those boys."

Supper was ready and waiting a good fifteen minutes, with Mamma's impatience visibly building up to the boiling point, before the study door opened and Mrs. Martin emerged, so resplendent in velvet and ostrich feathers that we all stared in awe. Only Papa was not noticeably impressed. He made the introduction with his customary ease. "Sister Martin, let me introduce Doctor White."

Doctor White beamed as he extended a hand that had obviously had no recent contact with soap and water. "Pleased to meetcha, Mrs. Martin. A widow lady, heh? Well, now, I sure know what it's like being alone. Soon's I got Red's letter I knowed it was the hand of fate resting on my shoulder."

Mrs. Martin barely touched his grimy hand, then turned away. She looked about the room a little wildly, her eyes going from Red to Rusty, both trying unsuccessfully to hide their disappointment. "Brother Reaves," she said acidly, "you have

78

two very talented boys. One is quite an artist, and the other one, it seems, writes very inspired letters."

It went right over Papa's head. But not Mamma's. The look she gave the boys as she banged the oven door was something to make their hearts quail.

Except for Papa and Doctor White, Mamma's good supper of fried ham, boiled potatoes, hot biscuit and gravy went begging that night. Mrs. Martin barely tasted her food but sat staring down at her plate, her cheeks blazing. My brothers were too miserable over the miscarriage of their plan to eat with their usual gusto, and I was too nervous at contemplating the probable punishment that awaited them to feel any real interest in food. Only the men seemed unaware of any tension. Doctor White talked volubly about the loneliness of a traveling man's life, emphasizing his remarks by gestures that kept us reminded of the neglected condition of his hands.

Just as Red and Rusty were about to escape from the table Mrs. Martin asked suddenly, "Brother Reaves, what time does that early-morning train run? I'd appreciate it if you'd take my trunks to the station. I really must be leaving."

That night I listened to Papa's voice from the other bed, after I was supposed to be asleep. "Easter, what do you suppose made Sister Martin get a sudden notion to leave? And what was that about Red writing a letter to Doctor White?"

"Nothing," Mamma answered emphatically, "absolutely nothing, Jim. Just a foolish joke. Now get to sleep because we've got to get up early. I sure don't want her missing that train."

And that was the last reference I heard to Red's attempt to play Cupid.

10

Mrs. Wilson and Mrs. Baker were at war again. Everyone in town knew that, after Mrs. Wilson's unsuccessful campaign to keep Mrs. Baker from being re-elected president of the Ladies' Aid and Mrs. Baker's retaliation by leaving Mrs. Wilson's name off all the committees she appointed. But I hadn't realized all the difficulties it made for Papa till the day I came home to find him discussing the situation with Mamma.

"Easter, she says she'll never set foot in the church again if we ask Mrs. Baker to take her place," he was saying. "But I don't know anybody else who can play. Do you?"

Mamma thought a moment, then she looked at me. A familiar gleam came into her eyes. "Jim, how long can Mrs. Wilson keep coming?"

Papa said hesitantly, giving me an uneasy glance, "Brother Wilson says maybe another month."

"That ought to be long enough." Mamma turned to me, "Ennen, you're going to start taking music lessons from Mrs. Wilson. Get your hands washed and we'll go over right now."

While Papa took care of the little girls, Mamma and I went across town to the Wilson home. Trudy and I were sent outside while the two women talked. Then I was called in and told that Mrs. Wilson had agreed to teach me to play hymns. If I'd apply myself I could take her place as church organist when she couldn't come. Did I want to try?

Mamma knew the answer to that. My chief delight was picking out tunes on our parlor organ, though I had had only about a year's music lessons before leaving Texas. Nothing would please me more than to be able to bring real melody out of that complicated arrangement of stops and black and white keys.

Every afternoon for a month I hurried directly to Mrs. Wilson's home and under her critical eye practiced the most familiar of the songs in the hymnal. I had a good ear for music, so Mrs. Wilson declared, and if I forgot just how a song went I could always fill in with a chord. By the end of my brief training period she had inspired me with considerable confidence, if not skill, and I could manage to keep my fingers moving over the keyboard and my feet pumping furiously at the same time—no small feat for even a trained musician.

I'm not sure who had the greater triumph the Wednesday night Mrs. Wilson publicly asked me to take her place at the organ. The glance she gave Mrs. Baker proclaimed her as the victor, but I can still see the surprised envy in the faces of the other girls my age when I marched up to take the coveted seat of honor.

Things didn't go off quite as smoothly as we'd expected, however. Papa meant well, but he overestimated my ability and calmly announced a number in which Mrs. Wilson hadn't drilled me.

It was a crisis I had to meet alone. A frantic glance at my coach showed her absorbed in exchanging glares with Mrs. Baker. Mamma was busy trying to make a sleepy Pugsy comfortable on the hard bench, so she proved no help at all. What had Mrs. Wilson said to do in such an emergency? *Strike a chord and hold it till the rough place is past.* So I struck a chord, putting all I had into the pumping so that the notes came loud and clear. The only trouble was, it was the wrong chord. Before I could switch keys Papa had swung into the song with enthusiasm, and I could never catch up with him.

Utterly unmindful of the disharmony we were creating, Papa sang to the end in a voice that shook the very rafters. Halfway through the first verse I gave up and sat in ignominious silence while Papa happily soloed, missing neither my support nor that of the confused congregation.

The next song did not go much better, though that was one I knew. I plunged into it with such enthusiasm that Papa never quite caught up with me. Altogether, I didn't feel my première as church organist had been all I'd wanted it to be, but Mrs. Wilson had a word of encouragement when she stopped me as I tried to dash out the back door of the church after the service.

"Don't you mind your papa, child. He never keeps time with me, either. And one thing about it, he sings so loud nobody can hear your mistakes."

Substituting for Mrs. Wilson until her baby was born, and pinch-hitting after that for years whenever someone with strong legs and willing hands was needed to make a noise if not music upon the organ, I learned to adjust to Papa and his peculiar style of singing. He had a heavy voice, with both tone quality and volume, but no respect for meter and harmony. To him, singing was an individual matter, merely an expression of the soul. If he was worried or upset his voice became a slow, impassioned plea, almost a dirge. If he was in a "God's in His heaven, all's right with the world" mood, you could brace yourself for a fast tempo that strained every pedal and wire in that wheezy reed instrument. But by summer and the beginning of the annual protracted meeting I had become almost skilled in reading Papa's face and disregarding the symbols printed in the book. Also in ignoring the fact that the mood of Brother John, the only man in the church who could approach Papa in volume, seldom matched Papa's moods.

The protracted meeting as we knew it had its own distinctive flavor—slight perhaps, but definite. For one thing, it was never organized in advance or circumscribed by time. It just began, sometimes with no more warning than a spring storm gave. And it ended as suddenly, when the visiting minister decided the "Spirit" was moving him on. That might be at the end of a week, or it might be after the meeting had gone on for a month or two. It was strictly in God's hands, as he told you at the beginning, and who could predict the moods of God? The very uncertainty of time made it important that no one miss a single service.

Besides, no such meeting was bound by denominational lines. A protracted meeting in progress at one church carried an obligation that members of all churches respected. Places of business were closed during the hours of the day service, and no Sunday morning or night or midweek service was held by any other church in town—Methodist, Presbyterian, or Campbellite, now known as the Christian Church. For the period of a protracted meeting all the churches united in a common effort to convert souls and save sinners.

The meeting that summer was conducted by a big, jolly man with a repertoire of stories that might have won him a contract on the stage. He was a new and fascinating species to me, for I had never before heard laughter and religion so well mixed. Tears and repentance, yes. Shouting and singing, certainly. But anecdotes and laughter when souls were threatened by hell fire? It was a novel and, I must admit, an appealing idea; but I couldn't shake off a feeling of guilt each time a giggle rose in me, and I was afraid to even glance toward Papa when a ripple of amusement ran through the congregation.

Mamma, I noticed, maintained a careful middle-of-the-fence position about Brother Carey's style of preaching. She didn't laugh at his jokes, but neither did she frown in disapproval. For Mamma to be noncommittal about anything was a novelty.

Of course the visiting minister stayed at the parsonage, though church members took turns inviting him into their homes for the two main meals of the day. Usually Papa was invited also, and sometimes Mamma, but the invitation never included her large brood, so she seldom went. Besides, there wasn't time, with all the extra washing and ironing for her family and the evangelist and the extra housecleaning and daily morning services, in addition to the huge breakfasts she must prepare and keep in the warming oven until her guest awoke, sometimes an hour or more after the family had finished.

My first insight into what Mamma really thought about the jocular minister came the morning Papa decided not to wait for Brother Carey to get up before making some calls on people "under conviction." Mamma turned from the stove with fire in her eyes. "You either wait or he don't eat," she said flatly. "It's enough to listen to his stories in the pulpit. I don't have to do it here."

But apparently the talents of Brother Carey as an entertainer were more appreciated by the town, for Papa reported that he drew the biggest crowds ever had at a protracted meeting, resulting in many new souls brought into the church. Among the new converts was Red, and I was so excited the

84

night he came to the mourner's bench that I got all mixed up and played the chorus of the invitational hymn again while Papa and the others were singing the second verse. And the next day I snubbed Trudy Wilson when she announced she had a new baby brother: "Well, I don't think I'd like a baby squalling around. I've got a brother who's been converted, and that's more than you've got."

Red and the rest of the new converts were baptized on a June Sunday afternoon, with most of the church members congregating on the riverbanks a mile from town to watch the rites.

Standing with the others, I had felt a deep trembling inside me as I watched the group of men and women and teen-age boys and girls walk slowly into the river until they stood before Papa, waist deep in water. The current looked so swift and so threatening as it swirled about their bodies. How could water so dirty wash away sins? Of course Papa had explained that there was no virtue in the water to bring salvation, but I hadn't wholly accepted that. Why else risk their very lives battling that swift current? Water terrified me, but it wasn't really for Red that I trembled that Sunday afternoon. It was for myself, for the day when my time would come to stand in midstream while Papa got ready to push me under that strangling river current. Such a day would come, I knew. Papa had already started offering prayers for my soul, and how could even God hold out against Papa's heaven-bound petitions? It was inevitable that some day the revengeful hand of God would be laid on me and I'd have to walk into that threatening river, like a sheep led to the slaughter. I shuddered all over at the very thought.

Rusty must have shared my dread, for that night I found him sitting on the back steps when he should have been asleep, forcing me to go all the way to the outhouse instead of stopping halfway along as I was in the habit of doing after night. When I came back he spoke to me abruptly.

"Skinny, let's you and me be smarter than Red. I don't want my head pushed down under that muddy old river."

"Neither do I," I said fervently. Then in a burst of confidence I added, "I don't even want to join the church, Rusty. I want to be wicked and some day write a book."

"A book?" Rusty's voice was scornful. "Who in heck wants to read a book? I'm going to paint pictures, that's what I'm going to do. With brushes and paints instead of just pencils."

Though not unappreciative of Rusty's talents, I felt rebuffed. "Who wants to set and look at pictures? What will you do with them after you paint them?"

"Hang them on the walls, stupid. Everybody has pictures hanging on their walls."

Everybody? I wondered. Not parsonages. All we had hanging on the walls was a framed, enlarged photograph of Mamma's parents, her most prized possession. But there were roses, a riot of red roses, on the wallpaper in the living room, pale yellow roses on the walls of the bedrooms. Why should anyone want to cover them over with pictures? I decided right then I didn't envy Rusty his talents. I'd keep my own. I'd write a book, whether or not anyone would read it.

11

Shortly after Mrs. Wilson's baby was born, she returned to her place as organist on Sunday. But for years I continued to play for the midweek service known as prayer meeting.

In our household, Wednesday night was just about as sacred as Sunday. More than once I wondered where the commandment about Wednesday night might be found. Certainly it was a dedicated evening, with none of us ever supplanting the church service with any school or social activity that might tempt us.

Actually, we preferred the Wednesday-night service because it was less formal than the Sunday worship and because Papa cut his hour-long sermon to a brief and impromptu talk. Also much time was devoted to singing, a feature that appealed strongly to Papa. Standing in front of his small congregation, his hands locked behind his back, he jumped from one favorite to another with such speed and enthusiasm that I'd usually be ending one number some time after he'd started another. The congregation, shifting step rapidly, confusedly trying to get in harmony with one or the other of us, often gave up altogether and let Papa solo blissfully.

After the singing and Papa's Bible talk, there were the testimonials, when most of the members present felt duty bound to testify for their Lord. Many of these became so routine that the regulars could anticipate each word that would be said, yet there was always the hope that someone might come up with a new and more or less stimulating thought, or afford opportunity for a little suppressed laughter. And there was always the testimony of Brother John, stereotyped but sure to arouse interest because Brother John's moods were so unpredictable.

Brother John was an elderly retired minister who definitely resented his status as a has-been and never missed an opportunity to make his presence known. Whether John was his Christian name or his surname I do not know, but I never heard him called anything else. Together with his meek little wife, he attended every service of any nature held in the church, with the exception of the Ladies' Aid. Once I heard Mamma say that the only reason she saw for attending the Ladies' Aid was that Brother John didn't, but I didn't know what she meant.

Brother John must have been a trial to poor Papa. He always sat in a certain seat, and if he arrived a few minutes late and found someone else occupying it he turned and stalked right out, his sad-faced wife obediently following. Only a stranger would be brash enough to take Brother John's seat, for all the members knew better. And after any such offense or other hurt to Brother John's sensitive feelings, Papa had to spend the better part of the week making peace overtures.

It was no small thing to Papa to have any disharmony in his church, and in his eyes anything that affected the peace of mind of one member affected the whole. He left no stone unturned to restore equanimity, from prayer to cajolery. When he inserted into his prayer at family altar time, "O, Lord, teach us Thy way of peace," I knew it was either Rusty in a fight again or Brother John in what Mamma flatly called a huff.

Papa took both with equal seriousness. Many a time he turned his pulpit over to Brother John, not because he felt his members would be given any elevating message but because he found it the only mode of appeasement acceptable to Brother John after his feelings had been ruffled by some thoughtless, or sometimes resentful, church member.

On Wednesday night, when Papa called for testimonials, everyone knew better than to speak before Brother John. His was the unquestioned right to arise first and testify for his Lord. Yet more often than not he was in no hurry. Papa would wait, the rest of us would wait, with only restlessly shuffling feet or a nervously cleared throat breaking the silence of the church. We kids would turn from our front-row bench and stare frankly, our eyes large with suspense, at the big man with the glistening bald head. We knew exactly what he would say when he arose, for he never varied his talk more than a word or two in the hundreds of times that we heard him. But we were never sure just how Brother John would approach his sacred moment. There was always the possibility that he might just get up and stalk out without saying anything. Or he might dissolve into tears, and to see a man do that always offered variety in an otherwise slightly routine service.

When he was ready, or felt the members had been sufficiently impressed, Brother John slowly and impressively arose, turned to face the audience with his hands folded across his huge paunch, and said in a solemn, hushed voice, "I thank the Lord He saved me when I was fourteen years old and has kept me in the straight and narrow way ever since. I've always done my duty, and in the fifty years my wife and I have been married we've never had a single cross word. Please God, He's got a home waiting for me in glory."

Once I heard Mamma say to Papa, indifferent to my presence, "It's easy to see why they've never had a cross word.

Likely she hasn't dared speak a half-dozen words in all those fifty years." And indeed, not once do I remember hearing Brother John's meek little wife say anything.

But in his more expansive moods Brother John did Papa a weekly service. Sister Stebbins sat on the opposite side of the building, and when Papa was really going strong with his sermon the Amens jumped back and forth across the room between her and Brother John like a bouncing tennis ball. What preacher wouldn't be encouraged by such approbation? At least, as Papa once said to Mamma, he didn't feel like he was talking to a blank wall.

Sister Stebbins, a thin, wiry woman who never appeared in public day or night without her slat sunbonnet, often became carried away by her spiritual fervor and shouted her praises to God without any inhibitions whatever.

Shouting was a common practice in the rural communities, but town churches like ours frowned on such lack of restraint as being irreverent. But when Sister Stebbins felt moved to shout, she shouted, and Brother John backed her up with his enthusiastic "Amen!" At such times Papa's beaming face expressed his approval too, though most of the members sat in such cold disapprobation that I often felt embarrassed for him and for Sister Stebbins.

Every fourth Wednesday night the singing and the testimonials were cut short to give time to the monthly business meeting of the church. This often proved very diverting to the younger generation also. A Baptist church was a democratic organization, and the members prized their right to express themselves on matters of church policy or business, and they held majority rule as one of their sacred precepts. Doubtless that is why a church business meeting could erupt into volcanic explosions without warning. The opportunity to express one's opinions and dictate policy often proved too tempting.

Almost no one missed a business meeting for fear something exciting might happen and then they would have to get it all at second hand. And exciting things often did happen. Such as the time Brother Rodman made the motion that fellowship be withdrawn from Brother and Sister A—— who were delinquent in their grocery bill. When Papa suggested that there might be legitimate reasons why the bill had been allowed to go unpaid, the groceryman stood firm. "I don't care what reasons they have. I can't fellowship with people that owe me money."

Fellowship was important in a small, struggling church. No one knew that better than Papa. I listened, fascinated, while he tried some expert fence-sitting as the members began to divide into two groups—those who felt financially secure enough to take the stand that all Christians met their obligations promptly, and those who argued for charity because they were not sure but what they might be in the place occupied by the A——s just any day.

In the end the side of charity won after Papa got off his fence and embarrassed me no end by saying, "Brother Rodman, I owe you money. Are you ready to withdraw fellowship from me? And the church, all of you, owe me back salary. Shall I refuse to continue to serve you?"

I couldn't see why Mamma looked so pleased with him, considering the humiliating confession.

Another time a member didn't fare so well. This one was reported as having been seen drinking intoxicating alcohol with a non-Christian. Brought before the church body to answer the charges, Brother B—— made no denial.

"Sure, we had a little drink together. But we didn't get drunk, so what's the fuss about?"

Sister Stebbins answered that. Most of the women in those days obeyed Paul's admonition to keep silent in the church, but every generation has produced its bold leaders, and Sister Stebbins must have had the soul and spirit of a feminist. Certainly no one dared try to silence her when she felt moved to speak.

"Our Good Book says to avoid even the appearance of evil," she declared. "Brother B—— blasphemed our Lord, and unless he gets down on his knees and asks forgiveness of God and this church, we can't hold any more fellowship with him."

She made it an ultimatum. We all held our breath, waiting to see poor Brother B—— fall to his knees in repentance. But plainly he didn't feel repentant. He tried diplomacy instead.

"Sister Stebbins, aren't you being a little hard on me? This was a special occasion, and after all our Lord Himself provided the wine for a wedding, remember."

The good sister pushed her bonnet back a trifle and pursed up her lips, a sure sign she was about to take a stand for what she called Right, spelled with a capital R. "There's nothing in my Bible says He drank any of it," she shouted. "No God-fearing Christian would put that vile cup to the lips he praises God with. Our Lord says 'Blessed are the pure in heart.' Brother B——, did you feel pure with that sinful lust in you, that evil craving in your soul?"

Brother B—— blinked, startled at her vehemence, as her voice rose higher and shriller, accompanied by an obbligato of Amens from Brother John.

"Pray, man, before your soul is forever doomed. Get down on your knees and ask for forgiveness before Satan gets such a grip on you he won't let go."

Brother B—— committed the unpardonable sin then, the act that robbed his soul of its church home. "I'll be d—— if I will," he yelled, and turned and rushed out.

There was nothing that even Papa could do then, though he tried. Fellowship was withdrawn from Brother B—— and after that if I saw him in time I crossed the street to avoid meeting him. Not because I felt any scorn for him but because I was embarrassed. How did you greet a man who has been turned out of the church? No one bothered to tell me.

12

Another stormy session occurred when a woman was charged with "conduct unbecoming a Christian wife," and the fact that she was my Sunday-school teacher made me feel involved.

Her husband made the accusation, stating in a hard, strained voice that neighbors had told him his wife entertained a man on at least two occasions, when the husband was absent from town. He angrily demanded that the church take action against her.

This woman, whom I shall call Mrs. C—— was much younger than her husband, and I thought very beautiful. My heart ached for her that night as she bowed her head and sobbed softly while her irate husband thundered, "Ask her! She can't deny it!"

Papa said, his voice warm with compassion, "Sister C——, I am sure this can be explained."

But Leona C—— only cried harder, and I thrilled when Mamma got up to go over and sit beside her, putting an arm about her shaking shoulders. But Mamma's action seemed to cause an explosion in Mr. C——.

"She's a faithless woman!" he shouted. "She lusts after men the minute my back is turned——

Papa interrupted him by ordering me and several girls my

age to go to the parsonage to wait until the meeting was over. We trailed out, mystified and terribly disappointed.

Mamma wouldn't answer my questions when she came home, but the next day at school Trudy gave me all the details, about which her mother had been more talkative.

"My mother says your mother acted awful. She got right up and said she didn't believe Mrs. C—— was bad, that if they wanted to turn out all the women who let men come to their homes when their husbands were away they'd better start with her because there were always men underfoot at the parsonage, though they weren't men she asked there, goodness knows."

It sounded too much like Mamma for me to entertain any doubts. Though trembling inside for poor Mamma, my curiosity wasn't satisfied. "What did Mr. C—— say then?"

"He got right up and shook his fist at your mother and said if she wanted to entertain men that was hers and Brother Reaves' business but he wasn't going to stand for his wife doing it. My mother says there's no telling what might have happened then if Brother Reaves hadn't started praying. He prayed so long everybody got tired enough to go home."

I knew that technique of Papa's too. "Then what happened?"

"Oh, they just voted to go home and wait till next time to decide. But my mother says there won't any decent people speak to her anymore."

It did no good to question Mamma again that night.

"I told you not to ask questions, Ennen. Some things we just don't talk about. Now set the supper table and don't let me hear another word about this."

But the matter of Mrs. C—— wasn't so easily dismissed. That night after the house was dark we were awakened by a knock at the door. When Papa made a light, pulled his pants up over his nightshirt, and went to answer, Leona C——

95

stumbled in, her pretty face blotched and swollen from crying, shivering with cold.

"He pushed me out of the house and locked me out, Brother Reaves," she sobbed. "I just didn't know where else to go."

By then Mamma was up, a quilt draped about her. "You did right to come here, Leona," she said. "Jim, you go into the study and sleep with that book peddler. She can sleep with me."

There wasn't much talking after Mamma had brought her guest a clean gown and ordered her to bed—just a few soft sobs, broken by low whispers I failed to hear in spite of straining. Then the rhythmic breathing of the two told me I wouldn't learn anything more that night. Yet I was too disturbed to go right to sleep. How could I explain this at school tomorrow? Hadn't Trudy said no decent people would even speak to Leona C——? Yet here she was in our home, and Mamma seemed unaware of the dreadful consequences she might be inviting.

Low voices awoke me the next morning. Opening one eye, I saw Mrs. C—— sitting on the side of the other bed in Mamma's best gown, the one she kept carefully put away in the bottom bureau drawer to be ready for sudden illness or death, along with the clean sheets she ironed especially well in anticipation of the same emergency.

The gown was almost too short for Leona C—— and the sleeves stopped halfway to her elbows, but I thought she looked awfully pretty with her dark hair loose about her face and her soft red lips puckered as if she might start crying again.

"He's just jealous, Sister Reaves," she was saying in a little-girl voice that brought a lump into my throat. "Every time a man looks at me he gets mad."

"Then why did you allow that man to come to your home? You must have known it would cause trouble."

What was Mamma saying? Did she believe Leona C—— was guilty? If so, why had she asked her to stay with us?

Mrs. C—— half-covered her face with her hands so that her voice was muffled but still distinct. "I just don't know, Sister Reaves. We haven't done anything bad. Please believe that. It's—it's just—well, you know how his wife is, always nagging at him and telling everybody how he mistreats her. He likes to come and talk to me, says I make him feel good just listening. And I—I guess I like talking to him too. Seems like I can say things to him that I can't to my husband. Oh, I know that sounds awful, and I don't blame you if you can't believe me."

Mamma was brushing her long brick-red hair, then winding it on top of her head and stabbing bone hairpins into the loose wad. "I can believe you," she said matter-of-factly. "But you know as well as I do how wrong you've been to let a married man come to you with his problems. Maybe there wasn't any evil in your mind or his, but you should have known there would be in other folks'. Now stop worrying and tell all this to your husband when he cools off and comes after you."

Leona C—— looked up, and her pale eyes were big and dark with fear. "But suppose he doesn't come, Sister Reaves? What—what will I do then?"

"He'll come." Mamma sounded very confident. "Soon as he gets tired of his own cooking he'll be after you."

But three days passed and Mr. C—— didn't come. Mrs. C—— was hollow-eyed and jumpy, and I knew she wasn't sleeping much, for I could hear her turning and sighing in the next bed. Papa looked more worried each day, and I understood why after Trudy told me everybody was mad at him and Mamma for keeping Leona C—— at the parsonage.

"They ought not to take sides between a man and his wife," Trudy said loftily, and I sensed that she was quoting her mother again. I wanted to tell Mamma what was being said, but how could I after she had forbidden me to bring up the subject of Mrs. C——'s marital troubles?

On Friday afternoon I hurried home to find Mamma's wash lying unfinished in the rinse water and herself not in sight. Investigation revealed the parlor doors were closed, and from behind them came the low murmur of voices. By pressing my ear against the door I could hear quite plainly.

"But you can't ask your wife to do that!" Papa was saying indignantly. "People will never forget or forgive if she publicly confesses she's been guilty of adultery."

"She can't come back unless she does." I recognized that voice as belonging to Mr. C——, and excitement filled me. "Everybody already knows she's been carrying on with L—— and that I asked to have her churched. Unless she publicly admits her sin and asks forgiveness, I'm not taking her back."

Then the outside door slammed, and there was no sound in the room for a minute but Mrs. C——'s low sobbing. Then her broken voice: "He means it, Brother Reaves. He'll never let me go back, and I don't know what's going to become of me."

I knew what Papa would say next: "Let us pray, Sister C——."

Listening expectantly for Papa to give God all the facts they had withheld from me, I pressed a little closer against the door. It opened quietly and suddenly, sending me sprawling to my knees. I had only a glimpse of Papa and Mrs. C—— kneeling before their chairs, then Mamma had yanked me out and shut the door again, looking almost as startled at being discovered tiptoeing out on Papa while he prayed as I was at being caught eavesdropping.

"Come help me get out that washing," she ordered. "Nobody's going to pray it on the line."

Supper was very late that night, and Mrs. C——, looking pale and wan, came into the kitchen to help Mamma. Suddenly she dropped the fork she was turning meat with, letting it fall to the floor and make a big grease spot, while she put her hands over her face again. "I'm going to do it, Sister Reaves," I heard her say. "I've made up my mind."

"But you can't!" Mamma protested. "Have you thought what it means to her as well as you?"

"I've thought about what it means if I don't." Leona C——'s voice had turned a little hard and defiant. "I want to go home, and John won't ever let me till I say he was right. I never knew him to give up on anything he sets his mind on. They can church me next Wednesday night if they want to. But I want John to take me back."

Mamma picked up the fork and, without washing it, started turning the meat, which told me how upset she was, even though she sounded calm enough when she spoke.

"Well, if you've made up your mind I guess there's nothing more to say."

Saturday was always a busy day, with clothes to iron and the house to clean and Sunday baking to do, not to mention baths to take, which meant an early supper so we could all have a chance to use the tub beside the kitchen stove. So it was positively electrifying to have Mamma suddenly come out of her room dressed up, telling me to watch the pies in the oven, finish the ironing, and look after Pugsy until she got back. Mamma going calling on Saturday afternoon, and with company in the house? I couldn't believe it.

She was gone a long time, and when she came back she

99

looked tired and discouraged. "Well, I tried," she told Papa when he came into the kitchen. "But I guess you were right, it wasn't a very good idea. Now you'd better start praying again."

With no idea of what Mamma was talking about, I knew from past experience that she usually tried action before prayer. At least I thought so then, but now I know Mamma was prayer in action. She called on her God within her stanch heart, while Papa prayed to a Power that ruled the universe. The difference in their approach was often confusing to us children, as well as to the adult members of Papa's congregation, who did not always follow Mamma's thinking any more than Papa did.

That night I stayed awake till Mamma came to bed, though it was very late, hoping she and Leona C—— would talk some more. My alertness paid off, but only in more confusion.

"Leona," I heard Mamma whisper, "I went to see her today and told her what you plan to do tomorrow."

There was a startled gasp, then the almost violent movement of the springs told me Mrs. C—— must have sat up in her surprise. "But why? Why would you do a thing like that, Sister Reaves?"

"Because I'd want somebody to warn me if a woman was going to publicly admit she had sinned with my husband. I told her what you said about not having done anything wrong and that I believed you, but that you meant to bring shame on her and her children as well as on yourself just to make your husband feel noble when he forgives you and takes you back. And I told her that it might be you couldn't go through with it if she could forgive you and be friends with you. That maybe you'd feel different——"

"But I'm doing it to get John back," came Leona C——'s

frantic whisper. "I can't feel any different about that. He might even divorce me if I don't. I can't let that happen."

"Suppose she divorces him? Have you thought what will happen to those children?"

"I don't care! I've got to think about myself!"

"Well, all right then." Mamma sighed, and I could tell by the creak of the spring that she had stood up. "But that's what's made all the trouble—everybody just thinking about themselves. But I'll go tell Jim he might as well go to sleep. No use praying about somebody who's determined to destroy herself."

Sunday morning, with all its bustle and hurry, left no time for speculation, not even after I answered the phone to take a mysterious message for Mamma that made her look very pleased when I relayed it. "This is Mrs. L——," the voice had said. "Tell your mother to please wait for me and I'll come by to go to church with them." Taking Dutch and Pugsy, I went on ahead, secretly hoping that Mrs. C—— would have a headache or something and not show up. The excitement had all worn off, leaving only worry about what people must be saying and thinking about Mamma.

Sunday school was over and church about to begin when Mamma and Mrs. C—— appeared, causing such a ripple of excitement through the congregation that I too turned to stare. A woman and three children were with them, and I recognized Mrs. L——, though she was not a member of our church. She was a querulous, unhappy-looking woman and her three small children looked as irritable as she did. Mamma picked out a bench where they could all sit together, though each of the women had to hold a child in her lap. Whispers filled the church, and I felt a coldness inside me at the thought of what might be going to happen.

Papa preached on forgiveness that morning, and I felt sure he was paving the way for Sister C——'s public confession. Sure enough, when he gave the usual invitation at the close of his sermon there was a stir beside Mamma and a woman arose and came down the aisle. Only it wasn't Mrs. C——, but Mrs. L——! Leona C—— still sat on the bench beside Mamma, each of them holding a sleeping L—— child.

Papa met the woman almost halfway, his face beaming as he took her hand and led her to the front row, where they sat down and talked. Mrs. Wilson had to play the invitational hymn through twice before Papa stood up to announce that Mrs. L—— had come forward to rededicate her life to the Lord Jesus Christ. "Sister L—— feels she has not been as good a wife and mother as she should be, and she asks the prayers of all here to give her strength to lead a better Christian life. Let us pray with her now."

That prayer, I felt, was a little unfair to God and surely unfair to the rest of us. It supplied no details at all, just merely reminded God that forgiveness came from Him and that we could not expect to be forgiven unless we also forgave. Or was he telling Mrs. L—— that? It would seem so, for when it ended she jumped up with tears streaming down her face and went straight to throw her arms about Leona C——.

"Forgive me, Leona." She spoke loud enough to be heard by most of the church. "And I'll never have an ugly, jealous thought again."

As Papa pronounced the benediction, the two women were still embracing and a lot of women were wiping their eyes.

We had just got home when Mr. C—— appeared, scowling but looking pleased at the same time. "You might as well come on home," he told his wife. "If Mrs. L—— can be mistaken, so can I."

As soon as the door closed behind them Mamma drew a

102

long sigh of relief. "Thank goodness, that's over. I couldn't have stood that poor thing's tears much longer. Jim, they're not likely to turn her out of the church now, are they?"

"Not likely." Papa put his arm about Mamma as he added, "The Good Book says blessed are the peacemakers, honey. I'm glad you brought those two women together."

Mamma didn't seem to hear him. "I wonder if she was really guilty of sinning. Do you think we'll ever know, Jim?"

Papa's reply made me think he hadn't heard Mamma. "Let him who is without sin cast the first stone," he said gravely. And then he added softly, "Easter, did I ever tell you that you're the best wife a preacher could have?"

That remark seemed more puzzling than anything, in view of all the criticism poor Mamma had been receiving.

13

The letter from Bud came early in the summer, asking Mamma to let Dutch and me return to Waco for a vacation visit. My oldest brother has not been counted as one of the sinners because he had married just before we moved and stayed behind in Texas. As Papa once put it, his eyes twinkling, "I have six living children and one married one."

Of course Bud had been too young to marry, and now at twenty he was the father of a son whom none of us had yet seen. It seemed a vague and incomprehensible thing that Mamma and Papa were grandparents and that at twelve I was an aunt. Laughable, too, that even small Pugsy was one. Sometimes it even seemed unreal to think of Bud and his wife, a beautiful girl we still called Miss Nellie because he had insisted we address her like that when he first began courting her, as members of the family.

But it was exciting to think of visiting in their home and seeing again the friends we'd had in Waco, so at once both Dutch and I set up a clamor to be allowed to go. Finally Mamma consented, and then began the thrilling preparations for our first train ride alone.

Over and over Mamma briefed me as to my conduct and

my responsibility for Dutch. We were to be quiet on the train and stay in our seats unless we just had to go to the women's room, and then I was not to let Dutch go alone. We must be careful to keep our skirts down over our knees and not talk to strangers. Especially strange men. Above all, we were not to accept anything from men or to let one persuade us to leave the train under any circumstances.

Mamma made these directives so emphatic that by the time the great day arrived I was a bundle of nerves, almost afraid to glance toward the men that Papa brought to the parsonage. Until then men had been just a part of the everyday world and unimportant. Now, suddenly, they were my enemies, something to be feared and avoided. The fact that I had no idea at all as to why they might have ulterior designs upon me only increased my apprehension.

Our train left around seven in the morning, which meant arising in the early dawn. Mamma cooked us a heavy breakfast, which we were too excited to eat, and packed us a big lunch of fried chicken and jelly sandwiches in a shoe box, adding two big slices of cake and two apples for an afternoon snack. We would get to Waco in time to eat supper with Bud and Miss Nellie.

Over and over Mamma told us to eat only our own food and not to buy anything from the news vender on the train. It wasn't safe, she insisted, for two young girls alone to allow a man to give them anything. There had been stories in the newspapers about a man who put dope in candy he sold children. I must not take any chances or expose Dutch to any possible danger.

I was tingling with conflicting emotions as the train began to roll on that summer day. Standing on the cinder island waving good-by to us was all the safe world I knew—Papa wildly brandishing his big black Stetson, Mamma wiping her eyes and trying to smile, Red holding up Pugsy to blow us kisses, and Rusty running beside the moving train and yelling something that was lost in the screech of the whistle. This was the world we were leaving.

Ahead of us lay unknown adventures and danger, for the coach was filled with men of all types. And men had now become a threatening menace with which I must cope all alone. Dutch, of course, didn't count. At eight, Dutch was only an added worry. A feeling of devastating homesickness filled me, and if there had been any way of getting off that train I would have welcomed it.

Dutch, however, was untroubled by fears and misgivings. But within a half-hour she remembered her untouched breakfast and announced that she was ready to eat. My protests that we had to wait till noon were ignored. "I'm hungry now. I'd just as soon be hungry at noon as now. I want to eat."

Dutch could always present reason and logic for getting her way. It couldn't have been more than eight-thirty when she had me convinced that it was as bad to be hungry one time as another. We opened the lunch box. By nine o'clock everything was consumed, even the apples that were to have been our stay-bit for the afternoon.

Blissfully full, Dutch lay back and slept while I forced myself to remain alertly on guard, acutely aware of danger every time a man glanced in our direction. Time dragged along, and by noon I was so homesick to see Mamma and Rusty that I had to fight against humiliating tears.

Dutch woke up and informed me she was hungry. When I paid no attention because I was lost in my own misery, she informed the whole coach. When I finally convinced her we had nothing left to eat, she broke into wild sobs. The sobs grew in volume as her hunger increased, for Dutch was not given to inhibitions. Soon the people all around us were taking turns trying to placate her, and to all of them Dutch tearfully explained that she was starving to death.

Fully aware that she was thoroughly enjoying the attention, I tried cajolery and threats with equal lack of success. At last my exasperation, increased by my own hunger pangs, drove me to shaking her as I demanded silence. This only increased sympathy for Dutch and brought down on my head the condemnation of the whole coach. One woman took up arms for my abused sister, telling me and all who would listen how cruel and heartless I was and just what she thought of a mother who would send two children on a day's journey without any food. She appealed to the conductor, who said there was nothing he could do but if someone wanted to get off when we stopped at Gainsville and buy us sandwiches at the Harvey House they could. A man volunteered, increasing my worry even though Dutch was temporarily mollified.

In due time the train stopped for the late lunch hour and a few passengers got off to eat. True to his word, the man who had pledged himself to do something about Dutch brought back a package, which he proffered to her. "Here's some sandwiches, little girl. You can give your sister one if you want to."

Dutch reached eagerly but I was quicker. Before her fingers touched the package I had grabbed it and tossed it through the open window. Hadn't I promised Mamma to protect her?

Understandably, the man was as incensed as Dutch. For a second he glared at me, and I cowered in my seat, fearful that he meant to strike me. Doubtless he was tempted, but he must have been a strong character. All he did was to demand why in hell I had done that. "Those sandwiches cost good money, you snotty brat," he added.

His anger was terrifying, but stanch in my determination not to endanger us I just turned a cold shoulder on him, dis-

107

daining to answer. But Dutch, in her indignation, could not be ignored. All the rest of the afternoon she sobbed heartbrokenly, with the passengers swarming around her, trying to placate her without arousing any more antagonism in me. One offered chewing gum, another fresh peaches, and still another a licorice stick as a peace offering—all of which I refused emphatically on Dutch's behalf, offering no explanation. How do you explain to a potential enemy, subtly plotting your downfall, that you do not trust him? You can only show your lack of faith, and I made a most thorough demonstration of that state of mind. Before the afternoon was over there could be no doubt left in anyone's mind but that I was a most distrustful child. And Miss Nellie probably never had more appreciative guests than the two at her late dinner table that night.

During that visit with Miss Nellie I learned a little more about what is commonly called the facts of life. Of course Mamma would not have approved had she known the methods by which such knowledge came to me, but I was careful to see that Mamma never heard about the books that Miss Nellie saw no harm in my reading. She had opened her brown eyes wide when I asked permission to read the ones I saw in her room. "I don't see any reason why not, child. It looks to me you're big enough to read anything I can."

Bless her tender heart, she probably never knew that she opened up a whole new world by introducing me to Charlotte Brontë and her contemporaries. I went to Waco a confused child, fearful without knowing what I feared. I took away a new understanding of the relationship between the sexes, gained through the love stories that had never been allowed in the parsonage. Of course my new knowledge was vague and distorted, but it provided something tangible to be on guard against. Men as a whole were no longer my enemies.

Now I knew I had only to fear the leering, villainous type who sought to seduce me through fawning flattery.

Although I was still ignorant of why men found women so desirable, it was a great relief to learn that love motivated them rather than a desire to harm. I even began to hope that one might make advances toward me on the homeward trip, so that I could employ the technique used by my newly discovered heroines and squash him with a haughty look or a disdainful gesture. Now I deeply regretted the wasted sandwiches. Certainly there had been no thwarted love in the face of that man. Only a thwarted desire to spank me.

My desire to be a writer crystallized during that visit, also. Now I knew what I could write about, though the knowledge bred in me a sense of guilt that told me my ambitions must stay a closely guarded dream. But some day I would draw glowing word pictures of beautiful heroines sacrificing all for love, of valiant men fighting for favors from the fair lady of their heart's desire.

It was on this same momentous visit that I saw my first automobile. One day Bud said that he had a holiday from work in order to see a horseless carriage parade down Main Street. Did Dutch and I want to go with him to see this wonder of the ages? Miss Nellie didn't think she should take the baby, who was suffering from a mild "summer complaint." Frankly, she just didn't believe there was such a thing as a horseless carriage, and she wanted us to go and tell her if it had actually run by its own power.

She wasn't alone in her skepticism, I found as we waited for the appearance of the phenomenon. The sidewalks were thronged with doubters, openly saying they wouldn't believe it until they saw it and maybe not then. As time passed and the summer heat increased, the crowd grew restless and I agreed in my heart with those who maintained that we had all been the victims of a hoax. But still we waited, reluctant to leave.

Finally a shout went up. "Here it comes!" And there it did come, threading its way throught the scattering crowd—the utterly impossible, the truly miraculous! A buggy without any shafts, rolling along on rubber-tired wheels and noisily breathing smoke. The sight struck terror into the hearts of the crowd, making some men turn pale and tremble and women scream and faint.

Awe-struck and breathless, the crowd fell back as the self-propelled buggy rolled along the cleared street at a terrific rate of speed that Bud later estimated must have been all of ten miles an hour. We were all still dazed with wonder and shock as we drove home to tell Miss Nellie the incredible thing we had seen.

After that I was eager to go home and give Rusty an account of the phenomenon, though certain he would not believe me. Sometimes I wasn't sure myself that I had really seen such a thing.

The train trip home was made without incident, partly because we started in the middle of the night and Dutch was too sleepy to eat the generous lunch Miss Nellie had provided until daylight came, and within a few hours after that we were home and could stuff to our hearts' content.

It was so good to be home that I didn't really care that neither Rusty nor Red believed my story about the horseless buggy. But I worried about Mamma. She seemed as well as usual, but she had grown enormously fat while we were away. I just couldn't understand how only a month could make such a difference in her.

Then one day the Ladies' Aid met at our house, and there seemed some strange secrecy connected with the meeting. Every woman arrived carrying a bundle, and after they were assembled in the parlor the door was closed in spite of the heat. Mamma told me to keep Dutch and Pugsy outside, making it sound important.

Dutch, as always, resented my efforts to curtail her liberty. In the middle of the session she made a dash into the house and ran straight for the parlor to see if refreshments were being served yet, with me hot on her heels. When she flung open the parlor door there were excited squeals from the women, then Mamma's grotesque figure was barring the way.

"Ennen, didn't I tell you to keep her outside?"

Dutch's pigtails provided a good handhold, and I dragged her away, screetching her protests over my rough methods. But over her shoulder I had caught a glimpse of a paper-strewn floor and women trying to cover objects in their laps.

All the rest of the day I mulled over the mystery, for when refreshment time did come and Mamma let us help her carry in the plates, all evidence of the mysterious packages had disappeared; even the floor was cleared of the papers I had seen. When I asked Mamma what had been in the parcels the women brought, her cheeks pinked a little. "What parcels, child? I declare, you do get the funniest notions."

The mystery was cleared the next day but in a world-shaking way. Mamma sent me with a bucket of fresh milk to an ill neighbor, and the woman asked me what we had over at our house, a baby brother or a baby sister.

I stared at her stupidly. "We haven't got either one."

"Oh, I thought it was here," she said. "I heard the Ladies' Aid gave your mother a baby shower yesterday."

The truth burst upon me then with staggering force. The parcels—Mamma's bulky figure. She was going to have a baby! But in one of Miss Nellie's books a woman died having a baby and the husband hated the child ever afterward. Was Mamma liable to die?

111

Hurrying home, I watched for a chance to sneak into the parlor alone and lift the lid of the quilt box Mamma kept in there, disguised with a chintz cover to look like a settee under the window. Sure enough, there lay the answer to the mystery of the parcels—tiny little dresses, soft knitted jackets, flannel gowns and slips. That left no room for doubt. It had to be true. But when? How? What would happen to her?

For several days I worried, wanting to ask Mamma but knowing she would not discuss such things with me. Trudy might know, having had a baby brother last year, but pride forbade my asking her. Suppose she laughed at my ignorance? Or told her mother about my shamelessness in bringing up such a subject and her mother told Mamma? No, I couldn't ask Trudy. I couldn't ask anyone.

A week later my anxiety turned to myself and became a paralyzing terror from which I could find no escape. For something unprecedented suddenly happened to me. Was I too going to have a baby? I could think of nothing else to account for the shameful change in my body functions.

For two days I tried to keep my ugly secret, but then Mamma's sharp eyes detected my misery and she questioned me. The result of that first confidential talk with my mother on matters pertaining to the intimate facts of life was that I was told to stop worrying and given a book to read, titled *What Every Young Girl Should Know*.

It told me much I needed to know, relieving my mind of its burden of shame and guilt. Yet it told almost nothing I wanted to know about babies. Since Mamma still hadn't mentioned her condition, I couldn't bring up the subject.

Two weeks later Papa woke me in the middle of the night. "Get the girls up and take them over to Mrs. Olsen's," he said. "Tell her Mamma is sick and will she please come."

Mamma, strangely enough, had moved into the study bed,

112

and I could hear smothered sounds from there, as though she was in pain. With cold, shaking hands I hauled Dutch and Pugsy out of bed and dragged them, protesting vehemently, to the Olsen house down the block. Though it was still August, my teeth chattered so I could hardly deliver Papa's message when I aroused Mamma's friend. She didn't seem to mind getting up in the night, but quickly showed us a bed we could use and hurried away.

The rest of the night I lay sleepless, tense with fear as I tried to imagine what might be going on at the parsonage but failing utterly. Shortly after daybreak I heard Mrs. Olsen return, so I got up and dressed and went into the kitchen in fear and trembling.

She greeted me smilingly. "Well, Ennen, you've got a new baby brother over at your house. Surprised?"

And so the seventh young sinner came to the parsonage to live. He was given a Christian name, of course, but anyone of us would have had to stop and think if asked what it was. For some reason of his own Rusty dubbed the newcomer Dodo, and Dodo he stayed.

14

The very first day of school that fall Rusty had a terrible fight. He came into the schoolroom with blood smeared over his face, his hands grimy and his shirt torn. Across the room I cringed in my seat, wishing miserably that the floor would open and swallow me. For facing us, looking at Rusty's unkempt appearance with sharply discerning eyes, was our new teacher, upon whom I had so wanted to make a good impression.

This year Rusty and I, for the first time, would be in the same room though in separate grades. A room had been added to the one-room high school building, and the sixth and seventh grades had been thrown together to form a grammar school. A woman from Illinois had been hired as our teacher, in spite of many parental misgivings about any woman being able to handle the unruly teen-agers—"such as Parson Reaves' wild kids."

Papa, having heard this doubt expressed, had lectured us severely on what a bad influence we were becoming and how our bad reputations were hurting the cause to which he was dedicated. I had promised tearfully to make the new teacher's job as pleasant as possible, but all attempts to get a promise out of Rusty failed. He was too basically honest to make a promise he knew he had no intention of keeping. Teachers, of whatever sex, were natural enemies in Rusty's eyes.

So the term had begun as I had feared it might. Standing before us was a homely woman of around forty, with such gentle eyes that I instinctively felt that she could never handle Rusty. But as those pale blue eyes moved over us I felt myself shrinking inwardly, feeling this stranger already sensed which one was Rusty, the troublemaker, and which the younger sister whose intense loyalty often brought catastrophe upon both their heads.

Then the new teacher smiled, making her plain face almost beautiful. "I am Miss Olga Brown, but I'd like to have you call me what my pupils have always done—Miss Brownie. I know what some of you are thinking—that I am an ugly old maid—and you are quite right. But that will not keep us from being good friends. I like you, and that means you will have to like me."

We all sat up and gave her full attention then. Here at least was a novel approach. Only Rusty appeared uninterested.

"Now," Miss Brownie said, "each of you please stand in turn and give me your name."

Things went smoothly until it was Rusty's turn. He just sat staring straight ahead, pretending he didn't know we were all waiting breathlessly, and my heart skipped a beat as I saw that his eyes were beginning to cross.

Miss Brownie waited a moment, her eyes barely touching his bloody face; then she said pleasantly, "You must be Rusty. Next boy, please."

It was five minutes before morning recess when Miss Brownie next spoke to Rusty. Then she said, smiling, "You look like you could use some water on your face, Rusty. I'll excuse you now, ahead of the others."

115

Without a word Rusty bolted out of the room, and I wondered miserably if he didn't mean to take advantage of Miss Brownie's kindness and leave school. But when recess ended Rusty was back in his seat, his face shining clean.

Within a week all of us were Miss Brownie's slaves—all but Rusty. He continued to be defiantly hostile, and nothing the teacher did or said pleased him. But she continued to ignore his attitude, his failure to do his homework, and the plain evidence of his having been in another fight. Miss Brownie let a whole month pass without once sending him to report to the superintendent, the usual method of punishment. But all of us knew that it was just a matter of time, that she couldn't keep on pretending ignorance of Rusty's antagonism.

Finally the day came. Rusty arrived at school a half-hour late and made no attempt to explain his tardiness. Miss Brownie told him he would have to remain after school.

Not wanting to go home and report that Rusty had keen kept in, I lingered outside the building, waiting in dread to hear the sounds that would tell me my brother was getting the long-overdue punishment he'd been asking for. When I didn't hear anything I crept to the window and peeked in. The sash was up enough so that I also could hear plainly.

Rusty still sat at his desk, staring straight ahead of him, while Miss Brownie stood before him, tears running down her face. While I gaped in surprise I heard her low voice saying:

"I've only wanted you to have as much faith in me as I have in you, Rusty. I know how bright and how talented you are, and I've wanted to be your friend. But you won't let me. Rusty, why don't you like me?"

Plainly confused by this approach, Rusty shuffled his feet and muttered uneasily, "Aw, heck, I haven't got anything against you, Miss Brownie."

"Then help me, Rusty," she pleaded. "You're a natural-born

116

leader and all the others look up to you. I do need your help if I am to succeed with this job. And I want to feel you trust me as I do you. I haven't even asked your reason for being so late this morning or why you had the fight yesterday——"

"I can tell you that," Rusty broke in defiantly. "I had to lick Johnny Akers for saying I was teacher's pet because you didn't keep me in for not bringing up my arithmetic problems."

"Then you weren't quite fair to Johnny," she told him. "Because you have been my favorite, you know." She reached over and touched his hair gently as she added, "I guess I've been more than a little partial to you since that first day when I saw you sitting here all blood-smeared, looking so angry at the world. Rusty, I think you're wonderful."

I couldn't believe my ears. Apparently Rusty couldn't either. He stared at Miss Brownie, who was blinking back tears and smiling at him. "Me?" he said incredulously. "Me—wonderful?"

"Yes, you. Shall I tell you a secret, Rusty? There are times, many of them, when I wish I could do like you do and wham everybody who displeases me. I don't blame you a bit for fighting so much. It's such a mixed-up world sometimes, and people say and do such stupid things. But fighting is stupid also, because it doesn't solve anything. People are just as stupid or whatever when the fight is over as when it began. Nothing is changed, and so you have to fight again and keep on fighting. So don't you see that is never an answer? Not for a smart boy like you."

I'd heard enough, and I ran for home, certain that Miss Brownie had overestimated Rusty's intelligence and her own powers of persuasion. But when Rusty got home he flew into his chores so quickly that I began to wonder. Then after supper he got out his books and went to work on problems long over-due on Miss Brownie's desk. My respect for her soared.

From that day on Rusty was a changed boy. He became a

model student, and his fights were so few and far between that it was as though a stranger had taken his place on the grounds. But at home he was still defiant and stubborn, and I had the feeling that there were two Rustys and that Mamma and Papa and the others didn't even know the one who recited so brilliantly at school, who put the drawings on the board for Miss Brownie at Thanksgiving, and who had organized the boys into a club called the MBL. It was a secret club, and Rusty swore me to silence before revealing what the letters stood for: "Miss Brownie's League, of course, stupid."

It was still two weeks before Christmas when the MBL members announced plans for a party during the holidays. The boys boasted that it was to be the biggest and finest party ever given in our school, with each boy inviting a girl of his choice. There were to be written invitations, and all the girls waited excitedly to see if they would be chosen. I did not expect an invitation because I had never shown any particular interest in any boy, but I wanted terribly to go to that party because it seemed so important to Rusty. He confided to me that he had turned in the name of Mattie Brooks, and I was a little shocked because she was a senior, two years older than Rusty, and a girl Red had been dating some.

The day before the holidays began, the coveted little white envelopes appeared on the favored girls' desks; and, wonder of wonders, there was one on mine. Opening it with trembling hands, I read: "Mister William Blake requests the honor of your company to the MBL party in the home of Mr. and Mrs. Joe Whitehead on December 28 at eight P.M." Miss Brownie boarded at the Whiteheads.

What did it matter that Mr. William Blake was only Billy, the boy down the block who spent the better part of his time at the parsonage? Fully aware that the invitation expressed as much loyalty toward Rusty as interest in me, it was none the less thrilling to have a part in all the happy plans. Without even consulting Mamma, I wrote a stilted note of acceptance. Then I began worrying for fear they might not let me go, and because I could not expect to have a new dress such as some of the girls were planning.

Christmas seemed unimportant that year, with the big party just around the corner. We talked about it so much that even Papa began to take an interest and ask questions. Where was it to be given? Was I sure there wouldn't be any dancing? And which one of my brothers was taking me?

When he learned that I was to have an escort in the person of one Mr. William Blake, he was greatly disturbed. For a few heart-stopping moments it appeared that I might not go after all.

"Easter, she's too young to be dating boys. I don't think we should let her go."

The thought of missing that party was anguish so deep I couldn't even contemplate it without dissolving into tears. Mamma took my part, and Papa was overruled. But nothing was quite the same after he had finished admonishing me not to permit any familiarities from Billy, nor encourage any advances on his part.

Until then Billy had been just one of Rusty's friends, a boy with whom I had romped all summer, played tag, and had rough-and-tumble fights on the lawn. But before Papa got through talking to me I had lost sight of the boy who had been such fun to have around and saw only a potential suitor whose romantic impulses might prove too strong for him in an unguarded moment.

The result was the most miserable evening I'd ever spent. From the moment Billy appeared at the front door, awkward and ill at ease in his new role, I was miserably self-conscious.

We had to walk several blocks, and neither of us could think of anything to say. All the time Papa's warning kept ringing through my mind, so that when Mr. William Blake gallantly touched my elbow to help me step up onto the board sidewalk I shrank away from him in revulsion. "Don't touch me," I cried, putting as much distance between us as the walk would allow. Poor Billy, who had chased me all around the yard the week before to wash my face in snow, was bewildered and hurt.

The party was humiliating because I was so tongue-tied all evening that even Billy stopped trying to give me any attention. I was now conscious of sex and confused it with love. I was in love, as suddenly as a spring storm strikes, and bitterly jealous of every girl to whom Billy spoke all evening.

Being in love was a devastating experience. For weeks I suffered as greatly as any heroine in Miss Nellie's books, for after the night of the party Billy shunned me as though I had something contagious. Night after night I cried myself to sleep, and I developed such a case of sniffles that Mamma threatened to try out Doctor White's Catarrh Cure on me.

Only Miss Brownie recognized the symptoms and understood. She kept me after school one day to find out why my usually good grades had fallen off. Before I knew it she had the whole story. But she didn't laugh. Instead she said quite seriously that if I planned to be a writer I must expect to suffer heartbreak. How could I write with understanding unless I knew about life? I should, then, mark Billy down as experience, put him out of my thoughts, and apply myself to the talent that was undoubtedly mine. Otherwise the world might lose a great writer.

My heart was light when I went home, my head in the clouds. Yet never again was I to enjoy my brothers' friends as I had, for after that I was always conscious of a word that stood between us—sex. Papa had hoped to help me avoid that snare, but instead he had pushed me into it. Instead of looking for fun, I began looking for experience, dramatizing the smallest incidents.

15

Rusty's reformation lasted until school was out for the summer vacation. It collapsed like a pricked balloon the day Miss Brownie told us good-by and said she would not be coming back in the fall because she had not been hired for another year. Within forty-eight hours Rusty had picked two fights with boys bigger than he, ridden Red's bicycle without permission, failed to do any of his chores, and flatly refused to go to Sunday school and church on Sunday morning. Never before had Rusty openly defied Papa's edicts, but that morning he was ready to fight back at a world that had betrayed him.

"I'm not going to that old church again," he yelled. "They're all a bunch of long-tongued old gossips. I know what they said about Miss Brownie so she didn't get her job back. And it's all a bunch of black lies. She never sweet-talked us boys like they say, and she didn't kiss any of us either. I hate all those old gossips, and I hate Mr. Olsen for listening to them. I hate everybody in the whole world but Miss Brownie, and if you make me go to church I just won't stay. I'll run away."

Papa was fighting temptation of his own, eyeing that broom handle, when Mamma interfered. "Let him stay home today.

After all, he won't get much out of the service, feeling like he does."

But it was the first service of the summer revival, and Papa was adamant. Rusty went to church, but he kept his threat not to stay. While Papa was preaching he walked out, went home for a change of clothing, and ran away.

Fear filled us all when Red discovered the missing clothes. Rusty had threatened to run away before, but none of us had thought he'd really do it. Red started out to look for him, assuring Mamma that he'd find him and bring him back, and saying grimly to Papa, "I hope you beat the tar out of him." Judging by Papa's face, I was afraid that was just what he might do.

For hours we all waited in growing fear, too disturbed to notice when Dodo pulled himself up at the churn until it overturned and gave him and the kitchen a milk bath. Dodo, who had golden curls and deep blue eyes, looked like a small cherub, but he could find as much trouble as the rest of us.

Red came back before night, having found no trace of Rusty. "Maybe he hopped a freight," he said worriedly. "He was always talking about doing it."

Mamma began to cry. "He's certain to be killed," she moaned. "I simply don't know what to do."

Neither, apparently, did Papa. "Easter, don't worry. The Lord will take care of him."

He said the words over and over, as he'd said similar words many times before, but the conviction grew in me that Papa didn't really believe what he was saying. He prayed, but he looked as worried when he got through as when he started.

Only Papa went to church that night. The rest of us had all cried ourselves sick. Again Dodo took advantage of the confusion by picking the daisies off my new hat and eating them.

Two days passed without any word from Rusty. Mamma's face was white and drawn, Papa's increasingly grim. The evangelist arrived and said with hearty reassurance that boys would be boys, but none of us found comfort in that thought. Then suddenly it seemed that poor Rusty was forgotten by everyone but Pugsy and me. Red began whistling about his chores again, Papa busied himself with the business of saving souls, and Mamma was her old self as she baked and cleaned and went to church, serenely indifferent about poor Rusty.

It hurt me terribly that I seemed to be the only one worrying any more. I cried all the harder because no one else cried, though I took care not to let Mamma see me. If she cared so little about Rusty, would she sympathize with my grief?

Pugsy shared my feelings. Every time we sat down at the table she looked around to ask, "Where's Rusty?" And Mamma always replied, "He'll be home soon. Eat your food, Pugsy." Then tears would fill my throat, making my food taste bitter. How could Mamma be so hardhearted?

On the fifth day Billy Blake stopped by, looking mysterious. He hung around for an hour, and I suspected he was waiting for a chance to speak to me alone but I didn't make it easy for him. I had long since recovered from my broken heart, but my pride was still tender.

Finally Billy got the chance to whisper to me that he'd had a note from Rusty, who had enclosed one for me. "Read it and burn it," he whispered dramatically, thrusting a half-sheet of rough tablet paper into my hand, then running.

The note was short but so exciting I could hardly control myself. "I got to see you, Skinny. Come to the party Friday night but don't tell nobody."

The significance of that message was terrific, for it meant that Rusty hadn't run off to the far ends of the earth, nor had he been killed. He was still close enough to return at will. It was a comforting thought, but in asking me to meet him at Norma Patton's birthday party, the only party I knew about, he had posed a big problem for me. Plainly, he had forgotten that the meeting had begun and that I wouldn't be permitted to go to the party. Nor would I even be expected.

What could I do? This was Friday, too late to get word to Rusty that he had asked the impossible of me, even if Billy knew how to reach him. Yet I had to see him, to find out what terrible things might be happening to him in his homeless condition. I simply had to see Rusty, which meant I had to go to that party, meeting or no meeting.

In desperation I appealed to Mamma. "I've got to go to Norma's birthday party tonight, Mamma. I've simply got to."

Mamma turned from her bread-kneading to look at me curiously. "Since when is a party so important? You know your papa expects you to go to church."

"But can't I go just this one time?" I pleaded. "Mrs. Wilson will be at church to play, and no one will miss me. Oh, please Mamma, say I can go just this once."

"You know I can't say that." But Mamma's voice was kind, as though she vaguely understood the desperate situation in which I found myself. "It's hard enough on Papa, with Rusty gone and everybody wondering about him," she went on. "He wouldn't stand for you not going."

She was right, of course. No use appealing to Papa. I couldn't tell him about that message without betraying Rusty. Neither could I fail my brother by not being at that party, which would be given outdoors, as were most summertime festivities. Somehow I knew that Rusty would be lingering in the shadow of the big trees that surrounded the Patton place, afraid to make an appearance for fear Papa would hear about it. "Don't tell nobody," he had written. Poor, poor Rusty. How would he feel if I failed to be there? This drama in which I was playing a part gripped my imagination so that before night I was sick with worry induced by the thought of my brother skulking in fear and desperate loneliness in the darkness, betrayed by the one person in the world he had thought he could depend upon.

Mamma seemed to have forgotten about the party. She searched my face with her sharp eyes as we sat down to the early supper the meeting made necessary. "Are you sick, child? Your eyes look feverish and you're not eating."

Here was a way out, and I grabbed at it. "I feel sick," I said, truthfully enough.

Mamma nodded. "You look like you're coming down with something. Maybe you'd best stay home tonight. We can't have you getting sick with a meeting on."

Papa was a little harder to convince, but he finally agreed that maybe I should go right to bed. He almost spoiled things by suggesting Dodo be left with me, but Mamma vetoed that. "She might as well go to church as worry with the baby. He can sleep there."

Mamma was making it all so easy for me that for a wild second I had the idea she wanted me to slip out and go to that party! Instantly I dismissed the thought and got into bed, groaning loudly. But the instant the door closed behind the family I was up and dressing madly, afraid to think what the consequences would be if Papa found out. If only Rusty came soon, so I could hurry home before church was over!

Norma and her mother looked so surprised to see me that I was embarrassed and didn't know how to explain being able to come. It was hard to take part in the games when I was engrossed in watching and listening for a signal from Rusty. Time passed, and it didn't come. Had it been just a joke? I was getting frantic, knowing I couldn't wait much longer, when at last I heard the low whistle, Rusty's special signal to me, that told me he was waiting beyond the lights from the lanterns.

Without even looking around to see if I was being observed, I made a dash for the trees.

Rusty grinned at sight of me, and he looked so brown and well that I felt betrayed after all the anguish I'd gone through. He hurriedly explained that he was staying at the Harmon farm five miles from town, helping with field work for his board. But he was getting tired of the strenuous labor and wanted to come home. Did Mamma and Papa want him back? Would they punish him for running away?

How could I tell him that Mamma and Papa seemed utterly indifferent about his fate, that his name hadn't been mentioned in days, and that no one but Pugsy and I appeared to miss him? Poor Rusty looked so unhappy and yet still so defiant as he stood there, kicking at a tree root with his bare brown toes, that I could only shake my head helplessly.

He said, half pleadingly, half belligerently, "Gee whiz, Skinny, can't you find out something? If they're still mad at me I'm not coming back. I don't want a licking."

"Maybe Papa will just pray over you," I said hopefully. "But the meeting's going on and you'll have to go to church if you come home."

"Well, maybe so. But, gosh, going to church ain't so bad sometimes. It was just that I was sore about Miss Brownie and all the nasty things folks said about her and that old Professor Olsen not giving her back her job."

We were silent a moment, wasting precious time. Then Rusty broke down all my resistance. "Gosh, Skinny, I ain't even got a bed to sleep in. I fork hay all day and sleep on it nights in the loft. And she can't cook as good as Mamma and there's flies and mosquitoes all over the place. I had to sneak out a horse to ride in here tonight and if he finds it out he'll raise Cain." He added, almost hopefully, "Maybe have me arrested for horse-stealing."

"I'll talk to Mamma," I said. "Maybe Papa will come and get you."

"Maybe he will." He brightened visibly at the thought. "But don't tell them that you saw me or anything like that. Just say that Billy or somebody told you where I was. You know, so they don't know I said to tell them."

I understood perfectly. "I'll try, Rusty. I won't tell I saw you."

He wanted to make sure. "Cross your heart and hope to die?"

I nodded solemnly. "Cross my heart and hope to die."

Hurrying home, I didn't fear the empty darkness for once, for I carried with me the vision of Rusty riding that lonely five miles on a stolen horse, maybe hastening to a fate worse than death. By the time I reached the parsonage I was so upset I didn't even notice that the church was dark and the house too well lighted—not until I slipped in and heard Papa's voice raised in prayer in the study.

Mamma was putting the three children to bed. She barely glanced toward my shaking figure. "You might have made it back a little earlier," she said crossly. "Your papa is terribly upset. But did you see Rusty, and is he ready to come home and behave himself?"

I burst into sobs. "How did you know?" I wailed. "I promised him I wouldn't tell. I crossed my heart."

"You didn't tell." Mamma finished pinning a dry diaper on Dodo, then straightened up. "Do you think Papa should go after him tomorrow?"

I nodded eagerly, too relieved to even cry. "He works all day and he hasn't even a bed to sleep on and he might go to jail for stealing a horse. Oh, Mama, please get Papa to go beg him to come home."

Mamma said all right and went into the study to tell Papa. I made record time in getting undressed and into bed, fairly willing myself to get to sleep before Papa came in. It was too good to be true, but Mamma hadn't even scolded me for slipping out to go to the party. I couldn't hope for that kind of luck with Papa.

Hours later I awoke, conscious of a nagging thought that had been mine as I fell asleep. Now it was startlingly clear. How had Mamma known about Rusty? And why hadn't she asked me where he was?

The mystery was cleared the next morning when I awoke to find Papa had already had his breakfast and had left to bring Rusty home. "But how did he know where to go?" I gasped, bewildered. "You didn't give me a chance to tell you."

Mamma gave me one of her secret smiles, the kind that always made me feel as if a door had been shut in my face. "Child, we've known where Rusty was ever since last Tuesday when Mr. Harmon sent word to us. All we've been waiting for was for him to get enough, and we figured he'd find a way to let you know when he did."

"Then—you knew why I had to go to the party?"

"I suspected it. I knew if it was that, you'd go the minute our backs were turned."

And I had thought them cruel because they had stopped worrying! Awe filled me as I went about the Saturday housework. Were parents like God, able to read your very thoughts?

16

Rusty was so glad to get home that he didn't raise any objections about attending the meeting, especially after Mattie Brooks started coming every night.

Besides, this summer's evangelist had an unusually interesting repertoire of stories, all based upon his life of sin before he became a Christian and gave up worldly pleasures. He made his former life sound very fascinating. Night after night he regaled us with exciting stories of sin involving wine, women, and song, so that I felt terribly sorry for anyone having to exchange such an exciting and adventurous life for the prosaic one of a preacher. Often tears rolled down the minister's cheeks as he recounted his past, and I was never quite sure whether he cried from remorse or regret over his loss. He did make sin sound so very glamorous!

God, however, he pictured as a wrathful judge waiting to inflict upon man his just punishment. Plainly this reformed sinner had deserted a way of life he found pleasant only in order to placate a God he knew would punish him with eternal hell fire if he didn't. Before the first week had ended, I decided the tears all came from regret.

Yet so vividly did the evangelist picture the punishment

that waited for those who did not get ready for the end of the world, which he declared was close at hand, that each time I heard him I was stirred by fear and dread, realizing that if the end of the world was actually approaching I should do something to insure my own safety. But caution kept me from making a decision. Was the world really coming to an end? If not, I didn't want to give up all my good times just yet. And the preacher might be mistaken—I hoped.

One afternoon Mamma told me she had baked a fresh peach pie, which she wanted me to take to a member who had been ill and unable to attend the services. I didn't mind the walk across town, for the way led past the home of Winnie Harper, my shadow who went everywhere with me.

On the way to the Almon house I admitted my fears to Winnie, and we agreed to ask Mrs. Almon, whom Papa said had an astounding knowledge of the Bible, what she thought about the possibility of the world coming to an end.

Mrs. Almon welcomed our question. There was no doubt about it; Judgment Day was right upon us. She took her Bible to show us proof after proof, pointing out how all the prophecies had been fulfilled. And only the night before she had been given a vision of the angel Gabriel, horn in hand, announcing that the day had dawned. She even read in the Bible the very words he had used: "Thy sun shall no more go down."

We were more than impressed. We were terrified. For over an hour we listened in fear and trembling while the woman in whom I had utter confidence read to us passages of Scripture that left no room for doubt. God was about to visit his wrath upon a sinful world, bringing about its total destruction.

We were two confused and shaken girls when we started home about a half-hour before sundown, our hearts pounding in terror. Our first glance as we left the house was toward the sun. Sure enough, it had turned blood red, just as one of the Biblical prophecies had said it would. And there was a stillness and a closeness in the air that made it hard for us to breathe.

"It's coming," Winnie said in a hollow voice. "We'd better run if we're going to make it home."

Taking a more fatalistic view, I had another suggestion. "What's the use going home if the end of the world is coming? We might just as well wait right here, Winnie."

We were then passing the Almon orchard, in which was a big, gnarled old apple tree, inviting in its accessibility. Crawling under the fence, we climbed into the low-hanging branches, too disturbed to even notice the tempting half-ripe fruit with which the limbs were loaded. Settling ourselves comfortably, we started to wait it out. Wasn't an apple tree as good a place as any to be found by the Lord when He appeared with his flaming sword of vengeance?

While we waited, we discussed in awed whispers the mysteries of life and death and Mrs. Almon's vision. We didn't need to put our fear into words. Each was aware of it in the other, each helplessly clutched in its embrace.

Winnie said tremulously, "Do you think Episcopalians will go to heaven, too, Ennen? I was baptized into the church when I was a baby."

"I don't know," I confessed. "Papa said one time that there were a lot of folks who thought they were going there who weren't. I guess maybe he meant either Catholics or Episcopalians."

"Trudy Wilson said she didn't want to go there if Catholics or niggers did." Winnie was shivering violently in spite of the warm summer air. "But what if they're in—in the other place too? Ennen, can you see the sun still?"

The sun had disappeared behind a thin cloud, painting the sky a flaming color that struck fresh terror into our souls. I had no doubt at all that something world-shaking was taking place, and suddenly I had an overwhelming desire to be at home, listening to Papa's heavy voice raised in prayer. I'd even welcome the chance to kneel, as much as I hated it. You should meet the end of the world on your knees, but how could you while perched on the limb of a tree?

"Maybe," I ventured, "we ought to pray. I know the Lord's Prayer by heart."

"I know that too," Winnie said, plainly welcoming something tangible to do. At once she recited it, word for word as I had been taught. I was struck with surprise that a girl baptized in the Episcopal faith when a baby knew the same prayer as did I, who had been reared in a church that vehemently denounced infant baptism.

That concluded, we waited again. Suddenly it was dusk, and we realized the sun had not set but had been lost in that cloud, now a menacing blot along the horizon. Winnie, easily excitable, began to be sick, and just as I was about to get up the courage to suggest we make a dash for home, there came an angry yell beneath us in a deep male voice. "Hey, get out of that tree, younguns!"

Winnie screamed, lost her balance, and went crashing to the ground in a shower of apples. I followed more slowly, realizing it was Mr. Almon and not the angel Gabriel we had to face. But it was a very angry Mr. Almon, who looked at me in unveiled hostility.

"Say, ain't you Parson Reaves' girl? Don't he teach you any better than to steal apples?"

"We weren't stealing your apples," I said feebly. "We were just waiting for the world to come to an end."

He didn't look impressed. "You sound like my wife," he snorted. "She's been setting around waiting for the end of the world for ten years now, but still she nags me all the time to buy her something new for the house."

He looked down at the heaving Winnie, surrounded by apples, and growled, "What's she so sick about if she hasn't been eating green apples? Now you two get on home before it's dark. Your folks is going to hear about this too. I'm plumb tired of having kids strip my trees before the fruit has a chance to turn."

It seemed a long way home, conscious as I now was of the lateness of the hour and thinking how angry Mamma would be that I'd left her to fix the supper and mind the baby without any help.

I found the house in utter confusion. Dodo was screaming in protest over a spanking he had gotten for playing in the slop bucket, Pugsy was wailing because she needed someone to take her to the outhouse, Dutch had dropped a plate while trying to set the table, and the potatoes had burned while Mamma answered the phone to listen to Mr. Almon's complaint about me stealing his apples.

Facing a wrathful God couldn't be much worse than facing Mamma when she was really angry, I decided. Before her tongue-lashing had ended I knew my Judgment Day had come, after all. There was absolutely nothing I could say in self-defense without inviting my brothers' ridicule, for Mr. Almon's "ten years" kept ringing in my ears.

Papa came in and added his lecture on the sin of dishonesty. Then he turned all the others against me by holding up supper while he prayed for my forgiveness. Before the tumult had died down, I was sure both God and Mrs. Almon had betrayed me.

Winnie's scare resulted in practical action on her part. The next day she attended services with me again and surprised me by going forward and giving the evangelist her hand to indicate she wanted to join the church. Papa was greatly disturbed, not wanting to be accused of proselyting. He cleared himself by going to have a talk with her parents, who promptly forbid Winnie adding another church membership to the one she already had.

Tearfully, Winnie confided in me. "We don't know for sure that Mrs. Almon isn't right and I just wanted to be safe. How do we know whether Episcopalians or Baptists will get to heaven?"

That red sun, so frightening in its appearance, had not been without significance. The next day it began raining, and it seemed as though the bottom had dropped out of the skies. The second night the church held only a handful of people, but the undaunted minister shouted out his vehement warning about the fiery destiny awaiting all sinners. It seemed to me, cringing under the lash of his voice, that he was pointing his finger and his words directly at me. The fear I had known the day before swelled in me until I felt physically ill.

The flooding rain continued for three days and nights. The streets became rivers, with water standing inches deep everywhere. No attempt was made to continue the services, but the zealous minister was not silenced. Morning and night he filled the parsonage with his triumphant voice, reminding us that we had a jealous God who would not be denied by sinful men without visiting his wrath upon them. Hadn't He destroyed Sodom and Gomorrah? Hadn't He sent a flood upon the earth in Noah's day and wiped out all but the godly ones chosen to carry on the race?

In spite of Papa's mild disapproval, the intrepid evangelist drove over the town during the daylight hours, sounding his warning to flee the wrath of God wherever he could find a listener. Fear grew and spread in the town until it became almost a tangible thing stalking the rain-washed streets.

135

17

It was Sunday again, the fourth day of the big rain, and we awoke to find the yard and the street covered with a foot of water that swirled about the house too swiftly and was too red and muddy to be just rainfall.

Papa, always an early riser, came in to wake Mamma, and his voice spread alarm through the house even as the phone began ringing to warn us that the creek had overflowed and threatened to inundate the town. We must prepare to leave our homes at once, for the river was also bank full and rising rapidly.

Our small town had been built in a narrow valley between a creek and a river. Normally the creek was only a sluggish, shallow stream that wound crookedly along at the foot of the hills bordering its farther bank, emptying into the river a mile below town. Only in times of extremely hard rain, when the river was too full for the creek to empty, did it become a threat. We had heard stories of times when West Town, the colored section nearest the creek, had been flooded, but the high waters had seldom risen as far as the main part of town.

Seeing that angry stream swirling through the yard and

remembering the evangelist's dire prophecies and Mrs. Almon's vision, I could feel my very bones melting in fear. Tremblingly I tried to help the smaller girls dress and to comb their hair, but it seemed a useless gesture. What did such things matter if the world was going to be washed away?

With all my heart I wished I had heeded the warnings given me and had taken some action to make my position with God more secure. Disturbed as I was, I didn't feel it possible to wrestle with Pugsy enough to get all the tangles out of her thick curls. It was simpler just to brush the top down smoothly, and to braid Dutch's hair without any brushing or combing. Braids covered a multitude of snarls.

By the time we were dressed and Mamma had hurriedly packed a change of clothing for each of us, the water was lapping at the top step. A few more inches would bring it into the house. Papa had tried to reach the barn to harness the horse to the buggy, but Mamma's yells had brought him back into the house after the water had almost washed him off his feet twice. The visiting minister, looking pale and shaken, had stood in water on the bottom step to reach out a helping hand to Papa.

Soon a boat arrived, but it couldn't reach the house because of the fence. Then the town marshal came on his horse, riding up beside the porch so that Mamma could climb on behind him. I lifted Dodo into her arms and handed up Pugsy to the marshal, and as they splashed away through the water I wondered dismally if I'd ever see any of them again.

At once another rider came, and Dutch and I got on behind him. By then Red had managed to get to the barn and bring the horse to rescue Papa and the evangelist. Rusty, preferring the spectacular, made his way to the picket fence and walked the railing until he could climb off into a boat.

All of the evacuees from the west side of town were taken

to the East Side, which was protected so far from the rising water by the railroad track that bisected the settlement, its fill serving as a levee. A number of Papa's church members lived on the East Side, among them the Wilsons. We were taken there, finding Mamma waiting on us, a part of a small crowd of refugees. Among them were Mrs. Baker and her gangling son. I felt something like shock at seeing the two bitter enemies working side by side in the kitchen to provide hot coffee and sandwiches for the wet, hungry people.

The rain had stopped, but the swollen creek kept rising. Suddenly it reached the railroad track and threatened to cross. The alarm was spread quickly, and work crews were hastily organized to add to the height of the fill, using dirt, brick, sacks of flour—anything water-resistant. By noon every able-bodied man and boy in town was working feverishly, among them Papa and the evangelist. In the crowded East Side homes women made gallons of coffee and tubs of sandwiches for the laboring men.

At the height of this excited activity the town marshal reported that his workers had been unable to rescue the West Town Negroes. Convinced that the end of the world had come, just as the evangelist had been saying, they had gathered in their one-room schoolhouse to wait for the end, refusing to get in the boats sent after them. The water was already waist deep in the building, he reported, and it was getting so swift in the low section that it was dangerous to take a boat in.

"But we can't let them stay there and drown," Papa protested. "We must do something."

The marshal shook his head. "I've done all I can, Brother Reaves. I'm not sending any men back to argue with them. It's too risky."

Papa laid down his shovel. "Then I'll go. They're human beings, the same as the rest of us."

He had appealed to the workers then for help, saying they'd need all the boats available. The men looked at each other and shook their heads. "We've got to stay on this job," they told him. "Those people had their chance and wouldn't take it. Likely they still won't."

It was the evangelist who gave Papa support. Laying down the shovel with which he'd been working as hard as though his eagerness to escape death matched that of the vilest of sinners, he said thoughtfully, "I guess I'd better go with you, Brother Reaves. Seems I'm the one that put the fear into them. Maybe I should try to take it out."

The Methodist minister volunteered to man the oars of the third boat, and the fleet took off, with Red added to the party of clergymen because he could swim a little, if need be, and none of the others could.

It was Red who told us about the rescue and how the evangelist risked his life scrambling through the window of the schoolhouse where the frightened Negroes stood on benches in water that reached above the minister's waist as he waded in.

"Save yourselves, people," Red and the others heard him shout. "God has repented and will not destroy the earth again. I have his word for it in my Bible."

Then he quoted to them God's covenant with Noah: "Neither shall all flesh be cut off any more by the waters of a flood; neither shall there any more be a flood to destroy the earth."

"God sent me to warn you all," he shouted, "because it's fitting that every man should get ready to die. But He also sent me down here to take you out so you can live to repent of your sins. Now, let's get these women and children into the boats first."

It was the minister, Red said, who passed out the wailing children and helped the frightened women climb safely into

139

the boats. Then he stayed behind with the men until a second trip had been made and all the shivering, wet Negroes were brought to the East Side and given shelter. Some said it was the husky Negro men, laboring all through the night, who kept the water from crossing the railroad until it slowly began to recede.

While we stayed at the Wilson home for three days, Mamma found time to comb the girls' hair herself and discovered what lay beneath those pigtails of Dutch's and the flaxen curls of Pugsy that were so smooth on top and so tangled beneath. My humiliation was complete when Trudy witnessed the application of the hairbrush to a portion of my anatomy not ordinarily associated with its use.

Trudy openly gloated over my downfall. "I never had a spanking in all my life," she said piously. "But I guess preachers' kids are always worse than others. That's what Mr. Almon said when he caught you stealing his apples."

Again I couldn't deny my guilt without admitting why I'd been in the apple tree. With the creek falling and the world about to be restored to its old order, I felt secure enough not to want that known, especially by Trudy.

But a week later I sat in the church, listening to the fiery evangelist shouting warnings about the dangers of procrastination, and all the old worry was back. Above the mournful singing of "There's a Great Day Coming," his voice boomed out: "Are you ready, sinners? What are you going to say to your Lord when you meet Him face to face? Where can you hide when He tears the heavens asunder and comes in all His pomp and glory to call you to account for your sins? Are you ready for that Judgment Day?"

Papa and the evangelist received me joyfully and made a place for me on the mourners' bench, so called because tears were a natural accompaniment of repentance, and without repentance there could not be salvation. Yet I did not feel particularly repentant, only afraid. So when Papa and the church members who came up to kneel and pray for us alternately beseeched me to give my heart to God and God to accept me into the fold, I sat in stoic silence, wondering what more was expected of me. Hadn't I presented myself as an indication of my willingness to strike a bargain with God? Was He going to turn me down? I felt no different than when I had come forward.

After an hour, during which all the other penitents had tearfully surrendered and left, Mamma came from her place beside the sleeping children and took my hand. "What are you waiting for, Ennen?" Her voice almost betrayed her impatience. "The Lord can't save you unless you let Him. It's your choice, so make up your mind and let's get these children home and into bed."

Practical, that was Mamma. Life hadn't permitted her to indulge in much sentimentality. But even in my perturbed state of mind I was conscious of the shock in the faces of those who had been kneeling beside my trembling body for an hour, imploring God's mercy for me.

Now Mamma made it all sound so simple. Impulsively I jumped up and gave the waiting preacher my hand. "I've decided," I said breathlessly. "I want to join the church."

Relief that my eternal safety was finally assured was so strong in me that I strutted a little as we went home. I know I gave Trudy Wilson a triumphant glance that must have influenced her to follow my example the next day. Then, unreasonably glad that I had been the trail-blazer this time, I went forward with the others to kneel beside her and ask God's mercy on her soul.

It was Rusty who reminded me that I still had a hazard to surmount before my road to salvation was entirely clear. "Gee wilikers, I hope you don't drown when Papa sticks your head under the water."

With something like shock I realized I hadn't escaped all the flood waters after all. That night I dreamed of strangling in muddy water and awoke so terrified I couldn't go back to sleep for hours. The dream persisted during the two weeks we waited for the river to get back to normal, and I became so cross and jumpy that Mamma finally questioned me, something she rarely did. The one thing Mamma most respected was the privacy of an individual's mind.

"Something's bothering you, child. Why don't you tell me? Maybe I can help you."

By then my burden of fear had become too great for me to feel any reluctance to discuss it. "I don't want to be baptized," I confessed. "I'm scared."

She nodded, as though she, intrepid soul that she was, quite understood such a fear. "I thought maybe that was it. I felt pretty much the same way, though I was sixteen. But I was more scared of freezing to death than drowning. It was winter-time in northern Kansas, and the river ice was so thick they had to chop a hole in it and help us down into the water. Then we had to drive two miles in those wet clothes to get home, and it only ten degrees above zero."

The picture she drew was so shocking that I began shivering violently. "But why?" I gasped. "Why didn't you wait till spring?"

She gave me a little, intimate smile, as though we shared a secret. "I guess for the same reason you were afraid to wait till you grew up to join the church. Who knew what might happen before spring? Besides, that ice bath didn't hurt me a bit, and I didn't get pneumonia riding home in my wet clothes. Want to knew why?"

I nodded, almost overcome with awe.

142

"Because I quit being afraid before the day came," she said quietly. "Pappy, your grandfather, told me the secret. 'No need to be worrying, Easter,' he said. 'The way it looks to me, if God can save you from hell He ought to be able to save you from pneumonia. And it's Him told you to get baptized, nobody else.'"

I found comfort in such sound logic, preferring the river to hell fire. Almost like magic my fears disappeared. When the big day came and I stood on the riverbank with Trudy and the other female candidates for baptism, while our mothers knelt behind a screen made by the long, full skirts of the women gathered to watch and carefully pinned our petticoats and skirts so they wouldn't float when we entered the water, I felt nothing worse than a slight dread of how I might look emerging from the water with my hair and clothes plastered to my body.

Then even that was forgotten as I stood before Papa with the water almost reaching my waist and heard his quiet directions about holding my breath as my face went under, of just when and how to bend my knees. "Just trust God and me," he said, "and hold to my hand."

Ilis hand was big and his arms were strong. It was all over so quickly I hadn't even time to gasp. Just the soft brushing of warm water across my face, like a caress, then I was upright again, and Papa's booming "Amen!" was my signal to let Trudy take my place.

She didn't fare so well. In a second of panic she grabbed Papa's coat instead of his hand, then let her breath out an instant too soon so that she came up choking and gasping. But I didn't laugh or feel superior. As though this shared experience bound us together in a new blood pact, I reached out and took her hand, my heart fairly swelling with love. Together we left the water and stood with our arms about each other as Mamma threw a light blanket about us to protect our modesty.

In that moment in the water I understood for the first time how Mrs. Wilson and Mrs. Baker could drop their enmity at will. It wasn't necessary to like someone in order to love him. I was finding Trudy still had the ability to arouse antagonism in me, but after she had once aroused my compassion, there was always a deep bond of friendship between us.

The following summer Papa held a protracted meeting that attracted the attention but not the approval of his church. Not even members of his family were asked to attend, since the services were held in the schoolhouse in West Town.

The announcement that their pastor planned to conduct a revival meeting and organize a church among the Negroes brought a chorus of mild protests from the church members, most of whom felt Papa was embarrassing them by such fraternization. He ignored them and went right ahead, announcing from his pulpit one Sunday morning that the meeting had been concluded and that he would perform baptismal rites for his dark-skinned converts the following Sunday afternoon if anyone cared to attend.

This, they all agreed, was going too far. To preach to the social outcasts was one thing, to baptize them quite another. By such action Papa would surely forfeit the respect of the town and do damage to the church. The deacons, urged on by irate members, came to try to dissuade him.

Papa heard them through, then firmly announced his intention of performing the river rites as planned. "My Lord never turned away any who came to Him for healing. Nor will I, his disciple, condemn a man because of the color of his skin. God looks only at the heart, and so should we."

Papa's stand caused so much comment that half the town

144

turned out the next Sunday to see the river ceremony. Red went along with Papa to drive for him, and Mamma let me accompany them after Papa had interceded in my behalf. Doubtless I was moved more by curiosity than religious fervor, as were the other onlookers, but it pleased Papa that I wanted to go.

The scene on the riverbank that summer day was striking. On the one side stood the small cluster of Negroes, while just across the river was a larger group of white people, who had driven upstream a mile to where they could ford in order to keep themselves entirely apart while they watched the rites.

Because we were with Papa, Red and I were of a necessity on the side of the colored folk, yet still apart as we watched from the buggy drawn up to one side. It was my first opportunity to see Negroes at worship, and I was deeply impressed at their uninhibited fervor. Their singing, little more than a high chant, had a primitive wildness about it that was almost frightening. As Papa waded into the river, followed by the dozen baptismal candidates, the weird chanting rose until it had the sound of a shout of victory.

A brief hush fell over the group as Papa raised his hand over the head of the first candidate, a big, husky man on whose bare shoulders the sun glistened as in a mirror. Then as Papa's deep voice boomed out, "In the name of the Father, the Son, and Holy Ghost," there was a wild shriek of pure hysteria from a woman standing near our buggy with a baby in her arms. "Praise the Lord! Praise the Lord!" she shouted, beginning to throw her body into contortions that terrified me. Then to my horror she lifted the baby high in her arms and tossed it straight into the river!

Papa, facing her, moved faster than I'd ever seen him. His body seemed to leap out of the water, his long arms catching the child in mid-air as an expert athlete might catch a ball. Then he waded to the bank and put the screaming infant back into its mother's arms.

"Sister," I heard him say sternly, "we don't practice infant baptism in our church. Take care to meet this responsibility God has given you in making you a mother."

The woman subsided like a pricked balloon, and quieted the baby's cries by putting it at her breast. I looked away hastily, but I had a feeling of kinship with that woman, for I knew what it was like to merit Papa's disapproval. Like facing God.

18

Early winter was the time of year when Papa began to look worried. The annual business meeting of the church was held in November, at which time a call was extended the pastor for another year—or else it was voted to appoint a pulpit committee to look about and spot candidates who might be willing to replace him.

This autumn Papa looked more worried than usual, for rumor had it that the pulpit committee had been unofficially selected. We all knew the reason why. Mamma wasn't getting along with the Ladies' Aid. At almost every weekly meeting something would arise about which Mamma felt compelled to express her opinion, and invariably Mamma's opinions offended someone, mostly because she was so frank about expressing them.

Her latest offense had started reverberations all through the church, mild amusement on the part of outsiders, and high tension in the parsonage. Goaded by accumulated bills due to the church's failure to collect Papa's salary, Mamma had attempted to give the women a lesson on the Biblical method of financing the church through tithing. She didn't get very far before the wife of a prosperous farmer stopped her.

"Sister Reaves, are you saying we should give a tenth of

all we make? Why, do you realize how much that would be for us? Mr. Womack made ten bales of cotton this year. We certainly can't afford to give the church the price of a whole bale."

Mamma told Papa that night that when she looked at the woman's plump, well-dressed figure and thought of the ten dollars a year the family had pledged to pay the church, something just exploded inside her. "No," she had said stiffly, "I don't suppose you can, Sister Womack. Judas Iscariot loved money more than he did his Lord, too."

Trouble developed in the parsonage when Papa thought Mamma should apologize to Mrs. Womack and Mamma flatly refused to do so. "I just told the truth," she said stubbornly. "They do love money more than they love the Lord or else they'd pay you decent wages."

Papa could be stubborn too. "I don't work for the people, Easter. I work for the Lord. We'll have to trust Him to provide for us."

It was Rusty who heartlessly deepened the furrow in poor Papa's brow. "You'd better start telling Him you want another job, Papa. I hear they've already picked out the pulpit committee."

When Rusty escaped without a reprimand for his irreverence, we knew how worried Papa really was. That night he rolled and tossed until I heard Mamma scolding gently. "Jim, why do you care so much? You can do as much good going back to Texas, where you'll be appreciated."

Papa's sigh stirred pity in me. "It's not that simple, Easter. This is the field the Lord sent me into. I can't turn my back on it, no matter how hard things get. It's you and the children I worry about. And the people here. They're good and they mean well. I hate to think I've failed them."

It was a long time before Mamma answered him, and then her voice held the note of resignation it took on when she knew she'd lost an argument. "I guess maybe that's the way the Lord felt about Judas, too."

It was only a week before the annual church meeting when Dutch took sick. Twenty-four hours later the doctor looked from her to Mamma and gravely shook his head. "She's got double pneumonia, Sister Reaves. It's going to be a fight to save her."

Mamma never wasted time in worry if she could see something to do. "Then let's start fighting," she said, her blue eyes ablaze. "She's been sick before and got well. She can again."

Another twenty-four hours and the doctor was ready to give up. Dutch's temperature had reached 103 and was still climbing. Even with the doors closed to the study, where Mamma had put her to insure quiet, we could hear her labored breathing. The hoarse, grating sound of it seemed to be tearing my heart open with remorse for all the impatient scoldings, the toe-rakings in the night, the angry hair-pulling when I had to groom her. My remorse turned to stunned grief when the tired doctor gave up. "I'm sorry, but there's nothing more we can do. It's just a matter of hours now."

Mamma turned on Papa then, her eyes a little wild. "Why do you just stand here and let her die? You always pray about everything. Why aren't you praying now?"

Papa put his arm about her, his face all broken with grief. "Easter, I can't pray any more. I've turned her over to God, and if He wants her He can take her. Last night I had a dream, so real it was like a vision. I saw an angel and the Devil fighting over our child, and I was afraid the Devil was going to win. So I prayed then and told God that if

He'd save her from Satan He could have her. So don't you see I can't take that back?"

But Mamma wouldn't give up. Dutch wasn't going to die, she said, no matter how many visions Papa had. He could stop praying if he wanted to, but she was going to keep right on.

Night came, and Dutch still clung to life, with Mamma hovering over her as though to ward off the Angel of Death with her bare hands. Papa paced the floor in agony, but not a word of prayer did we hear him say. It seemed incredible, for we all knew Dutch was his favorite, always able to wind him around her little finger. For Papa to give up and stop praying was earth-shaking, cataclysmic; but all we heard during those tension-filled hours was his low, anguished "Not our will but Thine, Father."

Watching his helpless resignation and seeing the fighting light in Mamma's eyes gave me the feeling I was watching another fight over poor little Dutch, one similar to Papa's vision. And when neighbors and church members brought in dishes of food, as they had been doing ever since the crisis had struck the parsonage, and asked me in whispers how Dutch was, I didn't know what to tell them. Papa said she was going to die, Mamma said she wasn't. Who could predict the outcome when those two strong wills clashed?

Though it was early in November, a bitter cold norther had struck the day before and a freezing rain had coated the world with a thin sheet of ice. Night fell early. When Mamma came out of the study to drink a cup of coffee soon after dark, she saw the light in the church. "What's going on at the church?" she asked, almost indifferently.

Papa told her, "It's a group of women who asked to sit up all night and pray for us."

"On a night like this? Why, it's slick as glass outside."

"I know, Easter, but they want to do something. I sent Red over to build them a fire."

Mamma set down her cup and went to get her coat from the nail behind the door. "I'm going to bring them over here. God can hear prayers said in a warm kitchen just as good as in a cold church."

She added, her voice breaking a little with its weight of pain and fear, "I'm thankful somebody is still praying for her and not just giving up."

I looked at Papa, thinking he would surely go with her across that dark, slippery yard. But Papa must have felt this was something Mamma had to do alone, for he made no move to follow her. With a glance at Red, who was watching Dodo and Pugsy, I grabbed up my coat and ran after Mamma. But if she was even aware of my shivering figure slipping and sliding beside her, she didn't betray it.

The church was bitter cold, for it took hours for the pot-bellied heater to warm that high-ceilinged structure. Four women were huddled about the stove, and my surprise was overwhelming when I saw that one of them was Mrs. Womack, whom Mamma had so recently offended.

Mamma didn't speak until she stood beside them. Then her voice held a humility utterly foreign to it. "Sisters, I'm grateful for your prayers. I think Mr. Reaves has given her up, just wanting God to have His will done. But I want my child to live, and I believe if you will all stay by me and keep praying that she will. But I'd like it better if you'd come to the parsonage where it's warmer."

She added words I'd never expected to hear from her, her tone leaving no room for doubt as to her sincerity. "It's your house, you know. It's your right to pray there as well as here."

With one accord the women rose and drew their fascinators over their heads for the walk across the yard. Mrs. Womack

151

paused to put a plump hand on Mamma's arm and say gently, "We're staying right with you, Sister Reaves. We're all mothers, and we know how you feel."

Mamma looked at her, blinked back tears, and gave the equivalent to the apology she'd said she wouldn't make. "Thank you, Sister Womack. You're a good woman to drive in two miles on a night like this to help us out."

All night the four women sat in the kitchen, taking turns praying aloud for Dutch. Much against my will, I was sent to bed with Dodo. I slept lightly, and every time I woke I heard the low murmur from the kitchen. But, though I strained to listen, I never heard Papa's deep bass joining in. The women had taken over the praying, and Papa was on the outside looking in. In my excited speculation over who would win, I almost forgot it was poor Dutch's life that was at stake.

In the early dawn Mrs. Womack shook me awake. "We're going home now," she whispered. "Your Mamma's sleeping, so don't let the children wake her up. The poor dear is plumb tuckered out."

I sat up, a little panicky. "But what about Dutch?"

A wide smile broke the soft roundness of her face. "Oh, her fever's down and she's sleeping easy. We pulled her right through the crisis two hours ago."

So Mamma and her allies had won! In my vast relief I was almost sorry for Papa and God. But not for long, not after I saw Papa's beaming face and heard his fervent prayer of thanks. I could only conclude then that Papa must have known all along that God didn't really want Dutch.

At the annual business meeting the next Sunday afternoon Papa was given a unanimous call for another year. And the president of the Ladies' Aid reported that the women had voted to hold a Christmas sociable at the parsonage to raise some of the pastor's back pay!

The Sunday after Thanksgiving Papa made his formal acceptance of the church's call for another year. The church was crowded, because many of the townspeople who were not members of his congregation had come to show their high regard and friendship for him.

Mamma had taken particular pains with his clothes, making sure his stiff-bosomed shirt was snowy white, with all its pleats laid smoothly in place, his shiny black trousers neatly pressed, and his long-tailed frock coat free of wrinkles and stains. And Papa had spent long hours in his study preparing the sermon that would launch him on his fourth pastoral year in the town.

He was happy that morning, partly because Dutch sat with Mamma and Pugsy and the baby; partly because he had once again been given assurance of love from those he loved and served; and partly, I'm sure, because of the peace and harmony that prevailed in the parsonage. For some time the sinners, large and small, had appeared to be sprouting wings.

When Papa was really happy he was happy all over. That meant trouble for the organist, as I well knew. Nothing could have stopped Papa from singing that morning, and he was so filled with grace that he was utterly indifferent as to what he sang. While poor Mrs. Wilson frantically jumped from song to song, Papa's voice boomed out joyously, always at least a half-stanza ahead of her, and at least once starting off on a different song altogether.

Papa's mood warned me to expect a long sermon, preceded by a long, long prayer. He had a lot to thank God for that day and he wouldn't overlook a detail. Also there were things he could best say to his members by relaying it first to God, as I well knew.

Standing beside his pulpit with his long legs a little apart and his eyes closed, Papa was telling God all about his plans for the church to establish a rural mission post when Dodo grew tired of sitting still, slipped out of Mamma's arms, and started down the aisle to try out his new-found legs.

Aware of the attention he might attract if interfered with, Mamma motioned me to wait until the prayer had ended. But by then the toddler had mounted the pulpit platform and headed straight for Papa, who was utterly unaware of his proximity.

Papa was imploring God to lay his hand on the people's hearts when he was startled by a loud snicker from the congregation. He faltered, then went on, not knowing that Dodo, having approached him from the rear, now stood upright between his legs, grinning impishly at the congregation.

"O, Lord, we implore Thy help," Papa prayed—and a ripple of laughter ran through the house, for just then Dodo grabbed Papa's coat tails and started swinging.

With a hasty "Amen," Papa looked down at the baby poking his impish face from between his legs and said in mild reproof, "The Lord God protects His own, so there is nothing I can do. Daughter, will you come and get this child?"

19

Only Mamma would have dared express her disapproval of Carry Nation to her face, formidable figure that she was just then. When Papa had the letter from the vigorous anti-saloon worker saying that our town was on her itinerary and that she would like to make an overnight stop among us, he was delighted. Mamma, however, frowned on the idea. "What does she think she can do here? We haven't got any saloons to bust up."

"She's a great woman, Easter, working for a great cause. We are honored that she can give time to us."

Papa's views seemed to be shared by most of the town, for there was a great flurry of excitement over the proposed visit of Mrs. Nation. All three ministers of the town met with the school superintendent to plan a suitable welcome and arrange for her address. Since saloons were prohibited in the Indian Territory by the government, this visit could not be classified as one of Carry's usual crusades; therefore it called for extra hospitality on the part of all the churches as proof that she had our moral support.

For almost a week I was the envy of all my class when it was announced that Mrs. Nation would stay at the Baptist parsonage. Her male secretary, who, she wrote, would accompany her, would be entertained by the Methodist pastor, whose parsonage home was smaller than ours and whose family was even larger. I enjoyed their envy and felt that I had earned it by the time Mamma had the house clean enough to suit her. For once the cooking would be minimized, for every woman in the church seemed to be planning her favorite dish. "I hope she likes cake," Mamma said, laughing. "Mrs. Wilson and Mrs. Baker both insisted upon sending in a cake, and I'm going to have to ask her to eat a piece of each kind so I can report to them how much she liked it."

Mamma's problems multiplied when two other women sent in pies as their bid for culinary honors, and a fifth added iced cupcakes. But Papa didn't have time to sympathize with her. He was having his own problems as chairman of the program committee, trying to decide who would be the favored few to share the spotlight with Carry Nation at her lecture, which was to be given in the Methodist church, since it was the largest in town.

Papa and the Methodist minister, it had been decided, would make up the official welcoming committee to meet the train, which got in about mid-afternoon. But most of the town appeared at the depot unofficially, Rusty and I among them, eager for a first glance at a figure who had attracted so much national attention.

My reaction was one of acute disappointment as a dumpy middle-aged woman in a severely plain black dress and small hat with ties under her full chin got off the train. She was followed by a huge Negro man whom we assumed to be her servant, since he carried her small telescope-type valise.

Mrs. Nation beamed at the crowd pushing each other for a glimpse of her. "Down with Demon Alcohol," she cried. "I can see this is a God-fearing Christian town."

Papa was just helping Mrs. Nation into the buggy, with the colored man bestowing her single piece of luggage in the back, when the Methodist pastor rushed up. "Mrs. Nation, what about your secretary? He is to stay with me but I can't find him."

The Negro man came around the buggy, smiling. "I'm Mrs. Nation's secretary, sir."

The minister, stunned by surprise, forgot diplomacy. "You?"

Carry Nation seemed to take that as a challenge. "He certainly is," she snapped. "And he's as good as any man, woman, or child in this town."

Papa recovered before the other parson did. "Of course he's welcome," he said heartily. "And I'll see that he has a comfortable place to stay."

Rusty and I, excitement lending wings to our feet, had already reached the house to break the news of Papa's predicament before Papa, Mrs. Nation, and the colored secretary arrived. By the time the buggy stopped before the gate, Rusty was halfway to West Town, carrying Mamma's message to the pastor of the African Baptist church that Papa had organized. He hastened to the parsonage and invited the Kansas visitor to be a guest in his home, and all might have gone smoothly from then on if Mrs. Nation had been content to let well enough alone.

She wasn't. All the rest of the afternoon, when a stream of visitors came through the parsonage doors to pay their respects to the noted lady of hatchet fame, she held forth on the sins of racial intolerance, interspersing her remarks with her views on the sins of smoking, dancing, card-playing, drinking, and bustle-wearing.

It was her tirade against bustles that proved to be the straw that broke down Mamma. After all Mrs. Olsen, our very dearest friend, wore a bustle, and she was suffering acute humiliation as she sat mute in the midst of the storm, unable to get up from her chair without betraying the evidence of her sinful nature.

"Mrs. Nation," Mamma said at last, "you've told us a lot of things you're against. Now why don't you tell us something you're for?"

The illustrious crusader had her answer ready. "I'm for destroying every den of vice in this country and for making all men equal, whatever their color. And as long as God gives me strength to fight, I'll fight against drinking and race prejudice. As for silly women who wear bustles, don't they know that if God had wanted them to have humps behind like a camel He'd have made them that way?"

By then Papa was giving Mamma distress signals, so she gave up and went to the kitchen.

I had joined her there to help finish the supper when Papa came in, his face creased in worried lines. "She insists on having her secretary at church tonight, Easter. The committee has all tried to talk her out of it, but we can't budge her. But you know what it's liable to start."

Everyone knew, even I, that feeling against the colored man appearing in the church would be strong. But none of us realized just how strong until we got to the church that night to hear the lecture. The secretary was waiting outside for us as we arrived, a little late due to Mrs. Nation's lengthy tirade against snuff-dippers and tobacco-chewers. Mamma, claiming Pugsy and Dodo had to be put to bed, had stayed at home in disgust.

The church was crowded, and again I felt a little thrill of pleasurable excitement as I followed in the rear of the procession that was headed by Papa, behind whom walked the lecturer and the big colored man. At sight of us, there was a stirring through the audience, a sibilant whispering sound, then a deadly silence. I had just sat down on the second row when I realized there was a great deal of movement in the church. Craning my head, I saw that everyone was leaving. Quietly, but definitely. Soon there were only the ministers and their families and Mr. and Mrs. Olsen and their two young children left.

Mrs. Nation cut short the ministers' embarrassed apologies. "I'm used to it," she said grimly. "But they can't stop me from talking. I'm giving my lecture whether there's anybody here to listen or not."

Give it she did, apparently undeleted, waving her famous hatchet as she talked. An hour later she produced a long scroll and made an impassioned plea for all the youth present to come forward and sign the pledge. Since there was no one present who could be classified as youth except the Methodist minister's son and myself, we went forward and dutifully signed our names where she indicated. As a reward she pinned on each of us a small pink coral hatchet, set with imitation chip diamonds, to which was attached a tiny bow of white ribbon.

"My work here," she announced dramatically at the close of the brief pinning service, "has not been in vain if I have saved two young lives from the evils of alcohol."

Shortly after we got back to the parsonage, Papa received a phone call. "Brother Reaves," an excited voice gasped, "a bunch of white men are beating up that man from Kansas."

Rusty and Red, who had managed to skip out of the lecture under cover of the general exodus, were right on Papa's heels as he dashed out of the house, as was Mrs. Nation. Mamma saw me in time to stop me. So I had to get my account at second hand.

"There were just two men," Rusty reported, "with that Negro hanging on to a lamppost between them. One would hit him on the side of the head, spinning him around toward the other, then that one would hit him and spin him back. Gee whiz, you ought to have seen everybody run when she came up waving her hatchet. Golly, she chased those men a block, and I bet if she could have caught them she'd have chopped off their heads."

I had no doubt whatever of that.

There was little sleep in the parsonage that night, or in the town. The battered Negro spent the night in our kitchen, holding beefsteak Mamma had planned to have for breakfast against his bruised face. Mrs. Nation stood guard over him, her hatchet on the ready, her angry voice rising and falling ceaselessly. Small bands of white men, I learned later, roamed the streets all night making threats against the frightened colored residents of West Town, who huddled in terror behind locked doors.

A half-hour before the north-bound train came in the next morning, the marshal, Mr. Olsen, and the other two ministers of the town appeared at our house, announcing that they had come to escort Mrs. Nation and her secretary to the depot. Mrs. Nation said flatly that she wasn't ready to leave just yet. That train went north, but she was headed for Texas and therefore would wait until the afternoon south-bound. It did no good for Papa and the marshal to point out that it wasn't safe for them to remain in town that long, that feeling was running high against them. Carry was adamant. "Nobody makes me run," she kept repeating. "I won't go till I'm ready."

Suddenly Mamma had reached another breaking point. "You make me sick," she cried. "Don't you know hate can do as much harm in the world as alcohol? You're not the friend of the colored people but their enemy when you turn folks against them like you did last night. If somebody had got

160

killed you would have been to blame, and all your preaching against everything wouldn't have changed it."

Carry must have decided she had met her match. A few minutes later she put on her funny little hat and announced she was ready to get out of a town in which the people were so narrow and bigoted. She didn't bother to say a word of praise about the cakes as she bid Mamma a curt good-by, but the colored man lingered a moment to thank her for the beefsteak. "You're right, madam," he said in a soft, cultured voice. "The race isn't always won by the fastest runner."

Rusty, hoping for more excitement, trailed the group to the depot, and he told me afterward how Mrs. Nation, subdued enough until the train was actually grinding to a stop beside her, suddenly went on the warpath again. A trainman had passed puffing on a pipe, and Carry had grabbed his arm. "My good man, don't you know that if God had intended you to smoke He would have made your nose turn up instead of down?"

20

Papa once visited in the home of a fellow Oklahoma minister while on a mission for the state Baptist Board. While the wife of his host prepared supper and the minister did his barn chores, Papa was entertained by the small son of the family.

"Where did you stay last night, Brother Reaves?"

Papa explained he'd missed a train and had to spend the night at a hotel.

The boy's eyes widened. "My!" he said. "Didn't that cost a lot of money?"

"It sure did, son. They charged me a dollar."

"That is a lot," the eight-year-old said gravely. "Seems like everything's going up these days but the preacher business."

And indeed a dollar was a lot to us on the outposts of civilization in the early 1900's. The frontier preacher, instead of being regarded as a public benefactor who merited just pay for his services, was something of a public charge, supported by volunteer donations from those who felt little responsibility for a man who had chosen to live his life thus.

Neither the minister of 1900–1905, or his family had any individual rights or private lives. They had been bought and paid for, but bought very cheaply. For working seven days a week and often far into the night; for traveling on foot or on horseback, in open vehicles or however he could cover distance; for exposing himself to every kind of weather without thought of personal comfort; for rushing to meet any need that might arise in the homes of his members and to arbitrate wherever friction reared its ugly head, Papa received the promise—seldom the pay—of fifty dollars a month. On that his family had to be clothed and fed and educated, donations made to charity, visitors to the parsonage entertained, and loans made to indigent members if needed. A preacher was a dedicated soul who worked for love, and who could put a valuation upon love?

The ministers themselves, Papa among them, were to blame for this attitude on the part of the people. He regarded his position as a sacred calling rather than as a profession, and felt that he profaned it by putting it on a business basis. One of my sharpest recollections is hearing Mamma try to persuade Papa to preach a sermon on the members' obligation in the matter of money and Papa's stern refusal. He did not work for men, he maintained. He was a servant of God, and as such he expected to make sacrifices. That his family must share in these sacrifices never struck him as anything but just and right. We too were servants of God, however unwillingly we might serve.

So strong was this belief in Papa that he never could feel he was due any pay for his work. Many times I heard him, with actual tears of gratitude in his eyes, thank a congregation for a meager payment on a long-overdue salary, acting as though he'd just been given a gift. It was only natural, then, that his members felt that any contribution on their part was a gesture of generosity for which they should be commended. Such as the man who nettled Mamma, when she and Papa were guests in his home, by bragging about his big-hearted-ness.

"I believe in paying my preacher," he told Mamma, after having just boasted that he made almost two hundred dollars a month, which made him wealthy by the standard of those days. "Even before I came to the Territory I gave my pastor five dollars a year, and I feel it's my duty to keep it up here, even though I don't do much running of the church."

A woman openly resented a lesson Mamma once gave on the subject of money at the Ladies' Aid. "My conscience is clear," she said emphatically. "If we gave any more to the church, we'd have to do without something we wanted our-selves."

"That's our trouble exactly," another hastened to agree. "We wouldn't mind giving if we had more than we needed our-selves. But we never do."

When Mamma came home, almost bursting with self-imposed restraint, she received small sympathy from Papa.

"Easter, we can't blame them. People should give because they want to, not because they feel they have to."

Mamma gave him a glare of frustration.

"Then you'd better find a way to make them want to or else we're going to get mighty hungry."

Papa's reply to that was his stock one. "We'll just have to trust in the Lord." And in general the loose system of financing a church employed by the Oklahoma preachers worked better than the skeptic might believe. When gifts were made they had only the motivation of love, never the pressure of duty, and the tie between the clergymen and their laymen was a close and sacred thing. I well remember being sent across town by Mamma to take milk or butter to a widow who supported herself and four children by taking in washing and ironing but who never failed to bring her offering of fifty cents

164

every Sunday. Papa could not refuse to accept it, so Mamma sent them small things when she could to make up for their too liberal contribution.

It wasn't unusual for members to make gifts to their minister, but we quickly learned that they expected full credit for it. Such as the time a man told Papa he had just dug his potatoes and had more than he could use, so if Papa would drive by his house he'd give him a bushel. Papa and the boys had made a good garden that year and we didn't particularly need potatoes, but Papa sent Red after them anyway, in order not to appear unappreciative. Red didn't get home until very late, and he was boiling mad then. He had worked two hours helping the man sort his crop of potatoes, under the pretense that he wanted to give only the best to his minister. Imagine Red's chagrin when the next statement of church finances was read at conference and this member was credited with paying Papa fifty cents on his salary, the price of one bushel of potatoes.

And there were the bees. A member kept an apiary in his orchard, and he learned on one of Papa's visits in his home that his pastor was very fond of honey. One day a wagon stopped at the parsonage, and the member came in to say he had brought Papa a hive of bees and where should he unload it. Papa was away, but all of us took an excited interest in this novel gift and it was finally located to everyone's satisfaction.

Papa was quite pleased with his gift and often anticipated the honey that might be his in the spring, even after he learned that he had been credited with receiving two dollars and a half on his back salary. The credit was for the hive, the good brother assured him; the bees were a gift. A gift with wings, it transpired.

Papa was again away on the day in early spring when the

bees swarmed and threatened to do a Rusty on us. On the advice of a neighbor we made the area hideous with noise, but the discontented bees refused to go back into their abandoned hive. When Papa got home he had an empty and useless beehive for which he'd been charged two-fifty, three disgusted youngsters nursing bee stings, a ruined new tin dishpan about which Mamma was more angry than about the loss of the bees, and a battered milk bucket.

On another occasion Papa proudly brought home a fresh ham a brother had "given" him. This meant good eating as long as it lasted, which wasn't long after two hungry preachers dropped in for an overnight visit and stayed three days. Later, when Papa brought Mamma his meager pay and explained sheepishly that three dollars had been deducted for the ham, Mamma wasn't surprised. But she was very disgusted. "And to think I fed it to those preachers," she said, "when every child in the house needs shoes."

Yet the church members did not always "horse-trade" with the pastor. There were many instances of unexpected kindnesses to balance the scales, in addition to the annual missionary boxes from which we salvaged most of our clothing and the occasional "poundings," which were not charged to Papa's account.

There were also instances of generous gifts, such as the new suit presented Papa by the church and made not deductible. This was the result of a bit of strategy on the part of Mamma and Aunt Mary, though they were never suspected.

Mamma was just starting to mend Papa's old coat, which was threatening to come apart at the elbow seams, when Aunt Mary took it out of her hands. "Let it alone," she said. "Don't try to mend it any more, Easter."

"But it's coming apart," Mamma exclaimed. "You know how Jim makes those sweeping gestures in the pulpit. I wouldn't dare let him wear it again like this."

"But that's what I'm telling you to do—dare to let them all see how badly he needs new clothes," Aunt Mary said indignantly. "Then maybe they'll raise the money due him. Please, Easter, just this once. Let's see what happens."

What happened was that on Saturday the chairman of the church's Territorial Mission Board stopped over, en route back to Guthrie from a trip to Texas. Mamma was so busy cooking for the illustrious visitor that she forgot Papa's neglected suit until he started to dress on Sunday morning. It was too late then to do anything, and she consoled herself with the thought that Papa wouldn't be preaching and so the worn suit would not be subjected to the strain of his gestures. Papa always invited any visiting clergyman to take his place in the pulpit.

What Mamma didn't know was that this ministerial visitor had developed a sore throat and declined to speak. So Papa preached as usual, except with a little added fervor because of his distinguished guest.

Mamma, torn with guilt and fear, watched helplessly as Papa began his usual arm-waving. Just as she feared, the strain was too great for the unmended coat. By the time he had really warmed up a patch of white was showing at the elbow, spreading slowly but surely up his arm. Before the sermon had ended Papa had rapt attention, but it was more for what, unknown to him, was happening to his coat than for his words of wisdom.

At the close of his sermon Papa introduced his illustrious guest, who rose slowly to his feet and fixed his eyes sternly on the congregation as he spoke briefly.

"I have heard good reports from this church, and so I wanted to stop over and see for myself what your needs, if any, were. I admit I am shocked at what I see."

Following the next Wednesday night services Papa was presented a box in which was a brand-new suit, a free gift from the church, a spokesman said. Papa was beaming his appreciation when Mamma just about spoiled things. "I don't think he can accept it," she said quietly. "It's a nice suit, and you all saw last Sunday how badly he needs it. But he wouldn't feel right going around so well dressed when his grocery bill hasn't been paid this month and he hasn't got feed in the barn for his hungry stock."

Within a week a special canvas of all the members had been made, and on Saturday Papa was given most of his neglected back salary. On Sunday he was resplendent in the new suit, and he preached with such vigor that I feared for it.

However, neither money nor clothes was important to Papa. He was so lacking in self-consciousness that he gave almost no thought to his personal appearance. More than once I shared in Mamma's acute humiliation when Papa appeared in the pulpit in a soiled shirt, having put on the one he had just taken off instead of the clean one laid out for him by Mamma. And unless we took care to guard against it, Papa was liable to pull out almost anything from his pocket to wipe his sweaty brow during his sermon. Once it was one of Mamma's red checked napkins, which he had carelessly stuffed into his pocket when leaving the table; once one of Mamma's cotton stockings; and once, I well remember, a none-too-clean diaper. One of my special tasks was to go through Papa's clothes after a visit in any home where he was served a meal, for the chances were good that Papa had absent-mindedly stuffed his hostess' best linen napkin into his pocket after eating.

One time Papa was late for a wedding he was to perform because he had lost his only clean collar and the black string tie Mamma had carefully placed in it. He searched, we all searched, but the articles had simply disappeared. At last Mamma found another collar, slightly frayed around the edges, and substituted a narrow black ribbon of hers for the tie. "Now get your hat and hurry," she admonished him, her patience exhausted. "I never in my life saw anybody could lose things as easy as you do."

Mamma was horrified when Papa returned after the ceremony with the lost collar and tie dangling from his pocket. But her horror grew as he sheepishly explained how it had come to be there: "It was around the crown of my hat, Easter. I never noticed it till I took off my hat to give it to Sister Hill and she started laughing."

The story got around, and everyone laughed over it—everyone but Mamma and me. Papa's absent-mindedness was no joking matter to us.

Neither was his indifference to money and material things, though with the years sharpening my perspective I can now see that Papa only obeyed his Lord's commandment and put first things first. Money was not important to him because it was secondary to service, and the rewards he valued most were not bankable. He had his dividends in the deep love of all who knew him, in warm friendships he made among rich and poor. Many of the most rewarding friendships were with men who denied the gospel so dear to Papa's heart.

Among these was a hard-crusted old farmer who lived close to town and who particularly distrusted those who took an open stand on religion. "Holy cheaters," he called them all, often vowing to Papa that he was the only person he'd ever known who lived his religion.

One day, during a particularly hard season, he stopped by the parsonage. "Mr. Reaves," he said, "you know I've got a good field of corn lying next to the road going past my place. I'm having to put a barbed-wire fence around it to keep out your thieving church members, but your legs are long enough to climb over. Any time you need corn, you just go out and help yourself."

Not all the gifts Papa received were things to eat. One that he treasured was a Bible, a modern translation, in which the inscription read, "From an ardent admirer of your sincerity." The name signed belonged to an agnostic who had the reputation of being the most unscrupulous lawyer in the Territory.

A confessed murderer, a member of one of the famed outlaw bands that operated in our part of the Territory, once stayed at the parsonage for three days while Papa awaited his decision to give himself up to the law.

And there was the woman of very questionable morals who found herself with no place to stay after getting off the train. Papa saw her sitting in the hotel lobby, learned of her plight, and invited her to go home with him, in spite of the hotel owner's frantic efforts to stop him. Perhaps in amusement, perhaps in desperation, the woman accepted his hospitality, but not under any false pretenses.

"Don't get any ideas about me and the preacher," she told Mamma, defiantly. "I haven't the faintest notion why he asked me here, but he did. If he's figuring on reforming me, he's wasting his time."

Mamma looked at the flashily dressed woman, whose paint-smeared lips and cheeks offended her very soul, and said quietly, "I doubt if he was thinking of doing anything but taking you in out of the cold night. Anybody that needs a bed is liable to be brought in by him, whether or not they deserve to be."

There were all kinds of characters in the long procession of visitors that passed through the doors of the parsonage. Men prominent in public life, men high in ecclesiastical work, men and women who were social outcasts, all received the same kind of treatment. Once there was a Mexican sheepherder whom Mamma was convinced was actually a Negro, though she never let him guess her suspicions. Papa had met the man, liked him, and invited him to spend the night. Such hospitality was second nature.

170

One day Papa visited in a rural district and came home with three orphan children who had been living with relatives when the home burned to the ground. Neighbors had given refuge to the couple and their children, but there was no room for the three young Joneses. Papa agreed to get them admitted to the Buckner Orphans' Home in Dallas, but they had to be cared for until it could be accomplished. So Mamma was elected, in spite of already having eight in the parsonage.

When Mamma looked stunned at sight of her woebegone small guests, Papa explained it all in one sentence. "They need a place to stay, Easter." To him, it was as simple as that. It was a month before they left, and Dutch, Mamma, and I all cried to see them go. I cried because the oldest girl went away in my best dress; I thought then that Mamma must be crying from pure joy to see them go; but I had no idea why Dutch cried unless it was because she'd have to go back to helping with the dishes, a job Allie Jones had taken over while she stayed with us.

After Papa took to preaching in rural districts on fifth Sundays and sometimes on weekdays, many of our guests were people from the farms who found travel so difficult over bad roads that they couldn't come to town without making an overnight stay. Among these, I remember, were two men who brought in a load of freshly dug sweet potatoes to market. But the potatoes proved to be a surplus commodity that year, and so for three days the two men stayed at the parsonage, coming in for each meal and feeding their team from Papa's meager store of feed. On the fourth day they gave up and drove away, taking the entire load of potatoes back home with them, without even offering Mamma a "mess" while she was cooking for them.

One of our visitors, a gray-haired missionary to the Indians, and a half-breed himself, was a favorite with us because he never sat at the table talking after he and Papa had eaten while we waited for second table. He pleased Mama by paying her a rare compliment.

"You know, Brother Reaves," he said one night, "our Lord was the only man ever perfect enough not to need a wife to balance his shortcomings. It's a good thing Sister Reaves has a level head to go with your soft heart."

21

Papa looked worried as he came into the kitchen. "I'm going over to the Watkinses'," he told Mamma. "They're having trouble. The old man's sick but he vows he's leaving home. I'll see what I can do."

The frontier missionary, such as Papa, often was called upon to arbitrate quarrels between members of a family, between members of his church, or between townspeople. Sometimes he had to act as both judge and jury and needed the wisdom of a Solomon to restore peace. Such a situation faced him at the home of these neighbors and church members, he reported to Mamma on his return home.

"They're terribly bitter at each other, Easter. As much as I can gather, it's all about who empties the slop jar. The old man claims he's sick and won't get out of bed, though she says he eats as much as ever and that he just wants to be waited on. He uses the vessel, claiming he isn't able to walk to the privy. She flatly refuses to empty it, claiming he isn't that sick."

Mamma laughed. "Well, it's nothing for you to worry about. Let them settle it."

"You don't understand, Easter. The vessel sets there unemptied, and it's making the house unfit to live in. But neither one of them will give in and carry it out."

Mamma threw up her arms in a gesture of impatience. "Jim, for pity's sake, haven't you got enough things to worry about without paying attention to a silly quarrel like that?"

"It isn't silly," Papa said gravely. "Anything that puts hate in the hearts of two people is important enough to do something about. Easter, you should see the way they look at each other and the tight hate in their voices when they speak, and after twenty years of marriage. The old man vows he's going to live with a daughter back East, but that won't work out. The family is poor and their house already crowded. Mrs. Watkins vows she should be the one to go, since she could help the daughter with the housework. And so they're at each other's throats about that and want me to decide who should leave and who should stay on here alone."

"Well? What did you tell them?"

But Mamma knew what his answer would be before he made it, as did we all. "I told them I'd pray about it. Something has to be done quick or else they'll both be sick."

"It strikes me they're both already sick in the head," Mamma said tartly. "What they really want is for you to decide who should empty that filthy slop jar."

Papa disappeared into his study and an hour later emerged, his face reposed. "How soon will supper be ready?" he asked, "I've got to go back to the Watkinses, but I won't be gone long."

Mamma controlled her curiosity until Papa came home. Supper was waiting, and he said a hasty grace and began eating with gusto, all traces of worry gone from his face. Finally Mamma said, much to my satisfaction, "Well, which one leaves home?"

Papa took another buttermilk biscuit before he answered.

"Neither one, I hope," he said gravely. "I have their promise to wait a week and try to work it out."

"A week? But they can't let that—that thing—set there a week! Which one will empty it?"

"It's emptied," Papa said complacently. "And I told Sister Watkins that if she'd not mention it to Ben again I'd come over every morning and see about it."

"You?" Mamma's tone registered horror. "You mean you emptied a filthy vessel for two able-bodied, stubborn old fools——"

"My Lord washed his disciples' feet," Papa said gently. "I'd just as soon do this for them, Easter."

Mamma drew in a deep breath, then let it out explosively. "Well, I give up. Just wait till this gets around town. They'll laugh in your face for being such a fool. Everybody knows old man Watkins just gets sick to get his own way about things."

"They laughed at my Lord. Let them laugh at me, I don't care. But I don't want them laughing at the Watkinses, so don't any of you say why I'm going over there every morning. It's nobody's business."

But the story got whispered around, as such things do in a small community. Each morning as Papa made his trip to the Watkinses' backhouse, windows all up and down the street were filled with the faces of watchers, some highly indignant that Papa should so demean his position, some equally angry with the Watkinses for permitting him to perform such a menial task, some only vastly amused at the whole situation.

It wasn't amusing to me. I felt disgraced, socially ostracized. I went to school with my head hanging in shame and became so sensitive that no one could laugh without my feeling that it involved me in some way. After her first efforts to dissuade him, Mamma had stopped discussing the Watkinses with Papa, blandly ignoring the whole thing. But it wasn't that simple for the rest of us. Rusty had two fights that week, and I strongly suspected they had something to do with Papa after a girl had called across the yard during recess to ask me if Papa was going to start cleaning privies next. For a minute I had actually envied Rusty his prowess with his fists.

The week of grace for the Watkinses lacked two days of being up when Papa came down with a terrible cold. Mamma put a mustard plaster on his chest and rubbed his throat with camphor and turpentine, but his fever persisted all night. When morning came she flatly refused to let him get out of bed. A cold October rain had set in, and he was staying inside and keeping dry if she had to tie him to the bed.

"Easter, I can't do it," he persisted hoarsely. "I've got to make at least one trip to the Watkinses'. I promised them."

"Well, that's one promise you won't keep. So you might as well stop your stewing, Jim. I won't let you get yourself sick just to make a couple of old fools feel important."

"Sometimes it's important to feel important," Papa argued. "That's the trouble with the Watkinses. Neither one feels important to the other one, and so they turn to hating each other. Easter, I've got to keep my word or they'll both lose faith in me."

"What you've got to do is stay in this bed and get over this cold." But at sight of the misery in his face she suddenly relented. "Jim, if it's that important to you, I'll go myself. I guess I can wash feet if you can."

And go Mamma did, hurrying off down the street right after breakfast while I stayed with Dodo and Pugsy.

She was back by the time I had combed Dutch's hair, but I was still struggling with my own and so overheard her report to Papa. "They wouldn't let me do it, Jim. He looked at me funny, like he was caught stealing something, when I went in and said I'd come in your place to empty the slop jar for them.

'I can't let you do something like that for me, Sister Reaves,' he said. I told him I wasn't doing it for him, that I was doing it for you, so you wouldn't make yourself sick. And then Mrs. Watkins jumped up and almost pushed me out the door. 'I don't guess you think any more of your man than I do mine,' she said, just like I had insulted her. 'He ain't sick and he knows it, but no woman is going to wait on him while I'm around. You tell Brother Reaves to stay in that bed till he's good and well and I'll look after this old fool I'm married to.'"

Mamma stopped, laughing merrily before going on. "Do you know what happened then, Jim? Mr. Watkins got right out of bed, and him with nothing on but his nightshirt, and went over and gave his wife a hug. 'I reckon I'm better, Gracie,' he said. 'A heap better, knowing you think that much of me after all. But I ain't letting no woman empty a slop jar after me. I'm carrying it out myself.'"

While I was marveling over that I heard Mamma add, her voice choked with laughter, "Do you know something, Jim? When I left they were arguing about which one would *let* the other one do it."

Which one won that argument I never knew. But it must have been an amicable settlement for the Watkinses were in church the following Sunday, beaming happily. When Papa gave the usual invitation they went forward, stating they wished to rededicate their lives and become active workers instead of the indifferent members they had been.

At one time Papa faced a crisis he didn't quite know how to handle when a newcomer to the town presented himself for church membership. Voting in new members was always a routine procedure when they came armed with a letter from another church, as did Mr. Harper and his wife. So that Sunday morning we were astounded to hear Papa hurriedly dismiss the congregation with the nice-looking couple standing there,

177

waiting to be voted in. "We'll have a business meeting Wednesday night and give Brother and Sister Harper the hand of fellowship next Sunday," he said, his face so red and uncomfortable-looking that I felt a stab of panic. Something was very wrong when Papa postponed offering the hand of fellowship to someone!

Mamma was troubled too, and Papa had no more than got in the house when she demanded to know what was wrong. "Jim, you never even voted those folks in. Why?"

"Easter, I just didn't know what to do. Harper is the man who came here to put in that pool hall, and I've already promised Brother Douglas I'd join him in preaching against it and getting it closed." Brother Douglas was the current pastor of the Methodist church and a fiery crusader against what he believed to be wrong. Poor Papa added helplessly, "I never dreamed the man was a church member and that he'd want to join my church."

Mamma was heartless enough to start laughing. "Well, it does look like you're in a corner. Either you lose a new member or quit being so chummy with that Methodist preacher."

But the problem, it developed, was more complex than that. Accepting into the church a man who owned a business held in such low repute as a public pool hall was not up to Papa but to the membership. Papa might have found a diplomatic way out of the dilemma if Brother John hadn't forced his hand Wednesday night. "Look here, Brother Reaves," he boomed, just as Papa was about to pronounce the benediction, "you don't aim to take into the church a man like that Harper fellow, do you?"

Papa looked about, as though hoping for a means of escape. "Now, Brother John," he said placatingly, "Mr. Harper seems like a good man. Let's pray about it——"

"Pray about it?" Brother John sounded scandalized. "Pray

178

to God about a man who runs a place of sin? That's plain blasphemy, Brother Reaves."

Someone ventured to come to Papa's aid, suggesting that a pool hall needn't necessarily be a sinful business. That brought a volley of objections. A large percentage of those present appeared to agree with Brother John that such places as pool halls should be banned from operating in decent communities and their owners ostracized by society. Before the dispute ended for the evening, tempers had exploded in a manner unfitting a church meeting and Brother John had delivered the flat ultimatum that the day a pool-hall owner was accepted into the membership of the church he would leave it, taking with him as many right-thinking people as he could.

In spite of Brother John's label of blasphemy, Papa prayed most of that night. He presented his problem to God again when he said grace at breakfast, and there was still so much he felt God should know before rendering His just decision that we ate cold biscuits and gravy.

In spite of Papa's pleas to the members not to discuss the problem publicly, word soon got about the town concerning the Baptists' quandary. That night a very indignant Mr. Harper appeared at the parsonage. Papa ushered him into his study. Then Rusty motioned me to follow him to his room, and I found that putting an ear against the door leading into the study was like having a grandstand seat.

"I'm an honest, respectable citizen and I run a decent business," Mr. Harper was telling Papa in a very emphatic tone. "I don't care for myself. To hell with your sanctimonious crowd. But I won't stand for my wife being insulted like this. I'll make a good paying member, better than some you've got. And I can make a mighty bad enemy when I'm forced to. I'm a man who fights for his rights, Brother Reaves."

I knew what Papa was going to say before he said it.

"Brother Harper, the kingdom of God is not taken by violence, nor can it be bought with money. Let us pray about this."

I had no way of knowing whether the pool-hall owner was praying or not, but there was no doubt about Papa. There were two occasions when he gave his voice full volume, and that was a lot of volume. One was when he talked long-distance over the telephone, shouting as though he would bridge the miles between him and his unseen party. The other was when he had a problem he felt needed the special attention of God. Then he apparently bridged the space between earth and heaven with his earnest voice, which rose and fell then like thunder rolling through the study.

Mr. Harper didn't have a chance to get in another word. He may even have tried, but he wasn't heard, unless it was by the listening ear of the Almighty. All we heard was Papa explaining to God about how there was always room in the fold for any sheep the Good Shepherd chose to bring in, but as keeper of the gates Papa couldn't take any chances on letting in wolves in sheep's clothing, which might scatter the fearful lambs and cause grief among the flock. He explained at length how the people felt about keeping the town free of dens of iniquity and sin, and reminded God that the pastor of the flock, of all men, could not condone such sinful occupations.

It was at this point that Papa was rudely interrupted, an unprecedented happening. Mr. Harper raised his voice until it was even louder than Papa's. "Now it's my turn," he shouted. "I can pray, too."

Sheer surprise must have silenced Papa, for then it was only Mr. Harper's voice raised in prayer. "Our Father in heaven, you've heard a lot of lies about me and the business I run. Everybody tells You it's a den of iniquity and that it will be a bad influence in the town and a lot of stuff like that. But I'm telling You it's no more wrong for a man to shoot pool than it is to knock a croquet ball around his front yard. I can promise You my place will be run wide open, with nobody trying to hide anything. And it will be closed on Sundays, like the rest of the business houses. And a tenth of all I make will be given to the church, like I've always done, provided You can talk sense into this bunch of stubborn old fools. And if You can't, then we'll join the Methodists and pay our money there."

A pause, so pregnant we could feel it through the wall; then Mr. Harper's angry, defiant "Amen." After a second the Amen was echoed by Papa, the very meekness of his tone indicating his defeat. Then there was the slamming of the door that told us we might as well get back to the dishes in the kitchen before Mamma missed us and investigated.

Papa was very thoughtful the rest of the evening, omitting any further reference to his problem during our family altar time or at breakfast-table grace the next morning. When we got home from school he was closeted in his study with a visitor, but that was not unusual enough to get any attention from us. Not until Mamma asked him, when he came into the kitchen where we were preparing supper, what the Methodist pastor had come to see him about.

"About that poolroom business," Papa admitted. "He heard about Harper trying to join our church, and he was scared I'd break my bargain with him to preach on the poolroom next Sunday."

Mamma waited for what appeared to be a reasonable time, then gently prodded Papa. "Well? What did you tell him? Are you going to do it?"

Papa looked at her in surprise. "Why, of course. I don't go back on my word, Easter."

Another wait, then our patience was rewarded. "Only thing is," Papa finally added, "I don't know what to say. I told Brother Douglas that neither one of us knew very much about pool halls since they're not places preachers go to, but if we are going to preach about one we ought to know what we're talking about. So"—he grinned in anticipation of Mamma's shock—"I challenged him to play a game with me between now and Sunday."

"You did what?" Mamma's horrified voice indicated that Papa's words had achieved the expected effect. "Jim, are you out of your mind? You'll have the whole church down on you if you go there."

"Maybe," Papa admitted. "But would that be any worse than me being down on a man without reason? Easter, all I know about pool-playing is what somebody has told me. Them saying it's a sin don't make it one in the eyes of God. All I want to do is see for myself what it's like."

"Well, is he going with you?"

Papa grinned again. "He said No till I told him the Harpers might try to join his church if we turned them down. Then he said he'd think it over."

Friday might turned out to be a memorable one for our town. On that night Papa and Mr. Douglas, dressed in their ministerial garb of frock coat, high winged collar, and black bow tie, walked into the new poolroom and announced they wanted to learn the game. Word of the proposed visit had leaked out, as such things do, and a considerable audience had gathered to witness this breaking of precedent, though most of them had taken up a safe stand on the sidewalk and street. Until the ministers' judgment was rendered, most of the men, even those not affiliated with either church, preferred to be considered neutral onlookers.

So it was an almost deserted place into which the two walked, to be greeted by the nervous owner, who didn't look as sure of himself as he had sounded the day he "prayed" in the study. Papa explained that they wanted to understand

182

the game so that they might pass only fair judgment, and Mr. Harper obligingly gave them cues and explained how their objective was to get the balls into the pockets. With men lining the walls and crowding the doors and windows to watch, the two preachers took their places at the table. Then Papa held up a hand as the nervous Methodist pastor took the stance suggested to make the first shot. "Let us pray, Brother Douglas."

Before his prayer was finished Papa had told God and the men of the town that the ministers were not there for worldly reasons or to placate any man. Their only objective was knowledge, their only desire to serve God. "All we do we do to Thy glory. Amen."

So, for the glory of God, the two ministers shot pool and Papa went down in inglorious defeat. The judgment he passed was understandable when he said in his sermon the next Sunday, "I see no more harm in this game than in knocking a croquet ball around the yard, but to me it seems a foolish waste of time."

That was Papa's only reference to the occasion that afforded the town so much amusement and answered his obligation to take a stand about the new enterprise. Following his sermon, he gave the usual invitation to prospective church members and added, beaming, "If Brother and Sister Harper will also present themselves, we will give them the hand of church and Christian fellowship."

"He'll make us a good member," I heard Papa tell Mamma later, and I knew he wasn't thinking of the tithe Brother Harper would bring in. "We need praying men in this church."

22

Another incident that called for arbitration had more serious aspects and came nearer home. It began when Farmer Case sent his oldest daughter, a pretty girl of seventeen, to stay at the parsonage until he could break off a romance between her and a hired hand he didn't want to dismiss until after the crops were laid by.

Jennie Case had dark brown eyes and round cheeks and a dimple when she laughed, and I thought she was marvelous. Even Mamma, who hadn't been consulted about having a guest for the summer, liked her and admitted she was good help about the house and with the children. Certainly while she was there the work got done with greater ease than I had thought possible. I was especially glad to have her company because Red and Rusty were both away that summer, working on a farm ten miles from town.

That Jennie nursed a broken heart made her all the more fascinating to a romantic girl of fourteen. At night we sat on the back steps and wished on the stars and Jennie cried a little as she talked about the man from whom she had been separated. Hank Beavers was wonderful, her dream lover, and some day they would be married, no matter what her cruel father said. It was true love between them and what could kill true love? Long after I went to bed I'd lie awake, making up stories in which Jennie was always the heroine, defying her tyrannical father for the sake of the man she loved with all her heart.

It was still July, with the heat waves dancing on roofs like ghostly sprites, when Mr. Case drove up one day for his daughter. "You can come on home now," he said tersely. "Your ma needs you to help with the fruit-canning and that scalawag's gone. I paid him off and sent him packing."

Jennie caught her breath, so sharply I heard her across the room. "Hank's gone?" she gasped, her round eyes going blank with shock. "Oh, no! He couldn't——"

"He was glad enough to go," her father said sharply. "I just told him we were both through with him and for him to hightail it out of the Territory. So now you can put him out of your mind and come on home and help your ma like a decent girl should."

Without a word Jennie turned and went to the boys' room, where she had been sleeping, to gather up her things. I followed, almost bursting with sympathy, and found her sitting on the edge of the bed, staring down at her clenched hands, unmindful of the large tears rolling down her cheeks. Her lips were moving but it was all I could do to hear the whispered words. "What will I do? What will I do?"

Taking her hand in mine, I was startled at how cold it was. "He'll come back, Jennie. I just know he'll come back for you."

There was dull despair in her eyes as she looked at me then. "No," she shocked me by saying, "he won't come back, ever."

A half-hour later Jennie was gone, leaving me only the consolation of her promise to return often to see us, a promise she never kept. The summer passed, and suddenly the boys were home and school had started again with all the hustle and bustle of getting off each morning.

October brought flaming color to the landscape; then we were crunching brown and red and gold leaves under our feet, with the trees standing stark and naked-looking against the sky. Still Jennie didn't come back, and suddenly she was just a figure in one of my dream stories, as though she had never really existed. I fell in love with an older man that fall, a young photographer who had just come to town and joined our church and was totally unaware of my crush on him. Rusty was in the throes of a violent affair with Mattie Brooks, keeping me supplied with full details of its progress, and Red was escorting a young second-grade teacher to town social affairs. Who needed anything to add color to dreams?

It was during the Christmas holidays, with the weather turning mildly warm as it often did before a fresh onslaught of winter, when Red came running in from the barn one morning, his eyes bugging with excitement. "Papa!" he yelled. "Come out here quick! There's a baby in your buggy."

Trooping to the barn at Red's flying heels, we could all hear the faint wailing before we reached the buggy. And there it was on the seat, snugly wrapped in a heavy patchwork quilt, its cries undoubtedly from hunger.

Back in the house Mamma unwrapped it gently, all the time vigorously expressing her indignation toward parties unknown. "Who in the world would do such an inhuman thing! And why us, of all people? Look, Jim, it's awfully young, maybe only a few hours old. Suppose it had died before we found it? How would its monster of a mother have felt then?"

The infant was dressed in an outing gown, its crocheted edging indicating that someone had made loving preparations for its coming. Its diaper was damp, so Mamma put on one of Dodo's, surrounded by a ring of curious faces. "A boy," she said softly. "Poor, poor little fellow, not to be wanted."

Because of the season and the fact that the baby had bright

red hair, we dubbed him Christmas and shortened it to Chris. All of us, from Red to Pugsy, voted to keep him, and likely we could have swung Papa over to our side if Mamma hadn't spoken so emphatically. "We will not. We've got all the mouths we can feed already. Jim, you'll have to get him in the orphans' home unless you can find someone in town who'll take him. Or else," she added angrily, "find the criminals that abandoned him to die."

That night the baby slept in a clothes basket beside Mamma's bed, and I could hear her getting up every little while to care for him. Papa had borrowed a bottle and a nipple from the drugstore, and warm milk from our cow had satisfied the baby's hunger. But he kept crying out, and Mamma kept crooning over him, "Poor little thing, poor little thing."

Once I heard her waken Papa, snoring gently beside her. "Jim, wake up and listen to me. I've just thought of something. Do you remember those dirty cousins, all full of bedbugs, that Herman Case sent in here to get rid of? Well, a man that would do that would do anything, it seems to me."

Papa was a long time answering her, but he sounded wide awake when he did. "Easter, you mustn't tell anyone what you're thinking. But I'll go out tomorrow and talk to him."

"He sent his girl in here to keep her away from that hired man," Mamma went on, her voice grim. "Only he was locking the stable door after the horse was gone. Remember how she got sick several times after eating?"

Papa said thoughtfully, "It could be. I seem to remember the man had red hair. But I didn't think Case would throw away his own blood kin."

"He didn't throw the child away. He just foisted him off on us, like he did the bedbugs. He knew we wouldn't let the little thing suffer."

I was so shocked I could hardly breathe. It was Jennie they

187

were talking about—Jennie and Hank Beavers! But it couldn't be true. Jennie wasn't that kind of girl, I thought frantically.

From the next bed I heard Mamma sigh. "Poor girl. She's not bad, Jim. Just foolish. Leaving this child here wasn't her idea, I'll guarantee."

"Easter, we mustn't jump to conclusions." Papa sounded as upset as I felt. "Wait till I talk to him."

When Papa got home the next night he looked so disturbed that Mamma didn't wait for me to be out of the room. "Well?" she asked. "Did you see her?"

Papa shook his head. "She's got the grippe. But we must be wrong, the way he acted. Threatened to shoot me if a word got out against her."

Mamma sent me in to set the table then, but I hurried back to the kitchen in time to hear her say, "I know you're right, Jim. We couldn't prove it, and talk would just hurt her. Least said soonest mended, I guess."

As word about Christmas spread over town, people began streaming to the parsonage to see him and conjecture about where he came from. I never heard Jennie's name mentioned, and gradually I relaxed, wanting to believe Mamma was wrong.

Papa wrote a letter to Buckner's Orphans' Home to ask them to take Christmas, and Mamma agreed, to our delight, to keep him until word came that he could be admitted.

Then Rusty came in one day with his clothes torn, his face blood-smeared, and his eyes still crossed. In answer to Mamma's indignant question he said belligerently, "I licked three kids. They said that baby was Papa's, that he had it put in our buggy. I made them eat their words."

There was shocked silence, with each of us afraid to look at the others. Then Mamma laughed, though it had a funny sound to it. "You shouldn't have paid any attention to that, Rusty. It's a silly thing for anybody to say."

Papa didn't say anything, not even to scold Rusty for fighting. Somehow I knew by his troubled face that the talk Rusty had heard wasn't new to him. He'd heard it too.

Mamma guessed also, but she didn't say anything until they were in bed, thinking me asleep. Then her voice sounded hard and angry, even in whispers.

"Did you know folks were saying that, Jim?"

"I heard it, Easter. But I thought it best to give it no importance."

"Well, it's important to me. Who do they say the mother is?"

"Jennie Case. Folks remember she stayed here last summer, and the neighbors say Case has kept her in hiding ever since. Then right after Christmas she got this grippe, only some don't think it's the grippe."

"Neither do I. Jim, what are we going to do? This talk has to be stopped."

"Easter, there's no way to stop talk but let it die down. Anything we do or say just gives folks more to talk about. If only I could see the girl . . . But Case won't let anyone near her, and he threatened me when I went out there. If I go back it'll just cause more talk."

"Maybe we can tell people about Hank Beavers."

"I've thought of that," Papa admitted. "But suppose the girl is innocent? Can we do that to her?"

Mamma sighed. "No, I suppose not. But tomorrow you'd better find somebody else to take care of the baby till we hear. At least folks won't be feeling quite so sorry for me then."

Papa said softly, "Bless you, honey. You're the best wife a man ever had."

The next day Papa came in to say the Watkinses down the

block had asked to keep the baby until a home was found for him. None of us protested when Mrs. Watkins came to get him, though Dutch and I both cried and Mamma looked as if she wanted to.

For the rest of the holidays Mamma spent all her spare time writing letters. At the end of the week Rusty mailed a stack so large it took almost a dollar to buy the stamps. "And all to Baptist preachers in Kansas," he reported to me. "Do you suppose Papa is trying to get another job?"

With all my heart I hoped he was. How could we continue to live here after this disgrace? I longed, too, to tell Rusty and everyone else about Hank Beavers, whom Jennie had loved. But always Papa's words stopped me. *Suppose the girl is innocent?* I didn't want to hurt Jennie more than she'd been hurt.

The holidays ended, and I went back to school with sick dread in my soul, shrinking cowardly from all the curious eyes of my schoolmates, my very flesh seeming to sear with shame when one of them questioned me about the baby. Of course I didn't doubt Papa, but what had faith in him to do with it? It was what others were thinking that made me suffer.

Trudy, with her usual frankness, did not spare me. "The church is split up," she said, seeming to relish the very taste of the words in her mouth. "Everyone is either on the 'tis or 'tain't side."

She added quickly, fearful I might not rise to her bait, "That means some say it is Brother Reaves' baby, some say it ain't. The 'tises say they won't come to hear him preach any more."

Judging from the diminished congregation the next Sunday, the 'tises were in the majority, but Papa preached with fire and passion on the sin of judging others. At home later Mamma told him that he wasted a lot of breath preaching to the ones that weren't there, but Papa just grinned.

190

"Maybe it wasn't wasted, Easter. Those who heard should have left feeling good about sins they hadn't committed."

During the next few weeks I could only guess at the pressure put upon Papa to reveal what he knew about baby Christmas, for even his most loyal supporters were convinced he knew more than he was telling. Over and over Papa's study door remained closed all evening, with only the low murmur of voices to tell us he had company. After such sessions Papa would roll and toss all night, maybe getting up to go back into his study to read and pray, if there was no guest in the bed.

One night when Mamma scolded him for not sleeping I heard him groan in pain, then say in his deep-throated whisper that was as clear as a shout, "Easter, they keep telling me the church is suffering, and I know it is. But is a group of people any more important than a single one of that group? Somehow I can't seem to feel it is."

Mamma's voice was almost impatient as she answered, "Jim, when you're doing what you feel is right your conscience ought to be clear enough to let you sleep. And if you can't, I wish you'd let me."

Mamma, I sometimes thought, was being very unfeeling about the whole thing, refusing to let any of us even bring up the subject. I couldn't understand that she was only trying to escape from evil by denying its power to hurt.

23

We had just started supper on a stormy Friday night in late January when there was a knock on the front door. Mamma looked at me.

"Go answer it. And I hope to goodness it's nobody wanting your papa to go out on a night like this."

When I opened the door a tall young man with bright red hair stepped inside. "I want to see the preacher," he said. Certain that it meant a wedding, I hurried back to the dining room to tell Papa.

Papa went into the front room, leaving the door open, and we heard the visitor introduce himself. "I'm Hank Beavers, sir. I got word through a Baptist preacher in my home town that you wanted to see me bad. What's it about? Is Jennie in trouble?"

Jennie's Hank! Suddenly my hand was shaking so that I had to lay down my fork. Afraid to look at Mamma, I knew her heart must be pounding like mine.

"I don't think her trouble is too bad," Papa was saying in the next room. "Come in and have supper with us and then we'll talk."

I jumped up for another plate, and then Papa was introducing Hank Beavers to all of us as though there was nothing unusual about his presence in the parsonage.

While he ate, the young man told of the trouble the minister in his town had gone to in trying to find him, and Papa grinned across the table at Mamma. "We had to write a lot of letters," he said to Hank Beavers, "not knowing anything about you except that you came from Kansas. We trusted one would reach you."

Hank gave him an anxious look. "You sure did want me bad," he said, laying down his fork. "I think, sir, if you don't mind we'd better get started on that talk."

They rose and went into Papa's study. A half-hour later Papa came out, smiling broadly. "Go hitch up the horse, Red. I've got a call to make."

Mamma said anxiously, "Can't it wait till morning, Jim?"

Papa shook his head. "It's waited too long now. But I've convinced Hank it might be best for me to go alone."

While Red hitched Papa's horse to the buggy, Mamma heated bricks and wrapped them in feed sacks, while I rummaged in the closet for an old blanket to throw over Papa's legs and found a muffler to tie about his ears. Thus entrenched against the biting cold, Papa set out on the four-mile round trip.

We had all gone to bed long before Papa got back, except for Mamma and Hank, who waited in the warm kitchen. His voice woke me, and I listened for a minute, then jumped out of bed and ran to the door to open it a crack, sure it had been Jennie's voice also that I heard. Sure enough, there she was in Hank's arms, laughing and crying and talking all at once.

"Oh, Hank, I didn't know what to do or where to write you. He said he'd kill you if you came back and he kept his loaded gun in the corner . . . But he said the baby had died, that I wasn't to tell anyone about it . . ."

All the time Hank was talking, too. "I never guessed, Jennie, darling. He said you didn't want to see me again and you didn't answer my letters——"

"I never saw any letters, Hank. Every day he told me what a fool I'd been to trust you. Now they say maybe our baby is alive and I don't even know if it's a boy or a girl——"

"I can tell you that," Mamma broke in, pouring coffee from the blackened pot on the stove. "He's a red-headed boy, the image of Hank. I've an idea the Watkinses are going to miss him when you take him away."

Jennie raised her face then, and the way she seemed to glow reminded me of the pictures of Jesus' mother on our Christmas Sunday-school cards. "Oh, Hank, can we? Can we?"

At once the glow left her face and she started crying again. "But he said he'd kill you if I saw you again. He means it, Hank. He won't let us be married."

Just then I saw Mamma looking my way, so I got back into bed, almost too happy to sleep. I still didn't understand everything, but I was sure now that Jennie wasn't bad. The glow I'd seen on her face told me that.

The next morning all was bustle and excitement in the parsonage. Papa was up early to build a fire in the parlor, seldom used for anything but weddings and Ladies' Aid meetings. Jennie and Hank were getting married, she told me with a glowing face, just as soon as Hank could get the license. Mamma wanted the kitchen clean and the beds made first, so we all hurried after Papa and Hank had left for town. Mamma sent Rusty to ask the Watkinses to come and bring Chris but not to tell anybody. All the time I could see how nervous Mamma was, and the way she kept looking out of the window.

"I'm scared, too," Jennie admitted, though the glow didn't

194

all leave her face. "He might not miss me till breakfast time, but he's sure to then."

"You mean he didn't know you were coming here?" We were making the beds, and I lost a precious second as I stopped to stare at her in growing excitement. "You— eloped?"

"I guess so." She giggled nervously. "Only I ran away with the preacher instead of the man I'm going to marry. You see I was in bed when Brother Reaves came to the farm last night, but I wasn't asleep. I heard his voice in the kitchen and I just knew he had come about me, so I sneaked to the door and listened and heard him tell Papa that Hank had come to marry me and take the baby. And all the time I had thought the baby died."

She stopped to wipe her eyes and I said impatiently, "Go on, Jennie. What happened then?"

"Well, Papa got awful mad and said the baby wasn't mine and that he'd kill anybody that said it was. He said he wouldn't let me marry Hank if he had wings because people would talk about us. I didn't wait to hear any more because I wanted to see Hank and I knew in my heart that the baby was ours, that Papa had brought it here because he knew Brother and Sister Reaves would take good care of it. So I dressed as quick as I could and climbed out of the bedroom window and got into Brother Reaves' buggy to wait till he came out of the house. I stayed down behind the seat so he didn't see me till he was halfway here, and then I got so cold I sneezed and he heard me."

Picturing Papa's surprise, I exclaimed excitedly, "What did Papa say when he saw you?"

"He said, 'The Lord's will be done.'"

About the time Papa and Hank got back, the Watkinses appeared with Christmas, in tears as Mamma had predicted.

But there wasn't time for Jennie to do more than touch the baby's bright hair, for we all knew Mr. Case should be there any minute. Rusty volunteered to watch at the back during the ceremony, to sound a warning if he should appear, while Red took up a station on the front stoop. The rest of us sat stiffly on parlor chairs to watch, Mamma holding baby Christmas.

Papa was just saying "I now pronounce you man and wife" when Rusty's shrill whistle came, followed an instant later by the slamming of the back door. Hank grabbed Jennie's hand as though he meant to run, but Papa stopped him. "Let us pray," he said sternly. No couple was really married in Papa's eyes without that prayer.

Hank hesitated, but Papa began praying, using all the familiar phrases I'd heard at other parsonage weddings. There were heavy footsteps coming through the kitchen, but Papa kept right on, though now I detected another note, also familiar. It was the intercessory tone he used when pleading for forgiveness for our sins, and I knew without looking up that Mr. Case stood in the door and that Papa knew it too.

At that it was a shock to open my eyes and see the sawed-off shotgun the farmer carried and the angry gleam in his eyes that said he was capable of using it. Did Papa see that too? If so, he ignored it, for he kept right on without a pause, while Mr. Case, maybe from habit, hesitated in the doorway, waiting for the prayer to end so he could start bloodletting.

But Papa was just getting started. He had a situation that called for praying and he meant to pray it through. On and on he went, with everyone else holding their breath as he unloaded all his burdened heart and all the sins of which mankind was guilty. If I hadn't known Papa better I would have

196

thought he was stalling for time, afraid to stop. Mr. Case shifted the gun and shuffled his feet and cleared his throat, but Papa prayed on, with Hank and Jennie standing with bowed heads and tightly clasped hands, afraid to look up.

It began to look like a marathon when suddenly the room exploded with a new sound that almost drowned out Papa's anguished voice. It was Christmas, and he was really mad.

Papa kept right on praying. "Lord, open our ears to hear Thy voice——"

But no one could hear anything except Christmas just then. Without waiting for Papa's "Amen," Mamma jumped up and spoke aloud, committing the unpardonable sin of blasphemy in Papa's eyes. "Oh, my, he must be hungry. I'll get his bottle."

To get to the kitchen she had to pass Mr. Case. Thrusting the yelling baby into his arms, right on top of the gun, Mamma said breathlessly, "Hold him a minute, Mr. Case."

For a breathless moment there was utter silence. Christmas stopped crying and Papa stopped praying so abruptly that his last word seemed to hang unfinished in the air. And Hank and Jennie stood as though paralyzed, staring at the man who held a gun and a baby at the same time.

Then Christmas made a funny sound, and Mr. Case looked down at him for a long moment. Then he said, wonderingly, "Sort of cute little feller, ain't he?"

Jennie burst into tears, and Hank put his arm about her, facing her father defiantly. Mamma hurried in with the bottle and took the baby. Mr. Case went over and carefully stood his gun in a corner. When he turned he had his handkerchief out and was loudly blowing his nose.

"I guess I've been an old fool," he said then.

Papa, as though just remembering he hadn't finished his prayer, said fervently, "Amen."

Mamma, sitting close to me, smiled down at little Chris and murmured softly, "I'm sorry I had to pinch you, baby. But he might have prayed all day if we hadn't done something."

News of the wedding spread fast, and the next day the church was crowded. Papa was at his best as he preached from the text that had been the keynote of his long prayer of the day before: "Let him who is without sin cast the first stone."

Afterward everybody crowded around to shake his hand, acting as though he'd been away a long time. And when we got home Papa beamed at Mamma happily.

"They're all good people, Easter. They won't remember or hold anything against me."

24

After that episode, life at the parsonage settled down to a slower tempo, but it was never actually dull. We sinners didn't permit it to be, in spite of the many restrictions Papa and his church members tried to place upon us.

Understanding and tolerant about most things, always charitable toward people, Papa could be most intolerant of the Devil and his wiles. One thing we could bank on was that the Devil would be the first blamed when we got out of hand or indulged in forbidden worldly pleasures. And there were few that weren't forbidden.

Dancing merited Papa's most violent condemnation. The Devil, he was convinced, had worked overtime thinking up that one. Any misguided soul who would be inveigled into such a sin had fallen right into Satan's trap.

Since square dancing, now more euphoniously known as folk dancing, was liable to be a part of any party or social gathering, the sinners not only had a problem but became a problem to those who would like to include us in their social festivities but did not want their fun limited by our restraints. More than once I was embarrassed by the whispered apologies of a hostess trying to explain to her other guests why dancing would not be a part of the evening's entertainment. And more than once I've had awkward apologies from a friend who had failed to invite me to her party. "You understand, we wanted to dance."

It wasn't enough that I fail to participate when there was dancing. Papa felt that my mere presence exposed me to sinful lusts of the flesh, a little like being exposed to smallpox or measles. So whenever we went to any social gathering it was under strict orders to leave if dancing began, and all our friends knew this.

To compensate us for what we couldn't do, Rusty and I sharpened our wits to think of things we might do that fell within the law, or of ways to outwit Papa in breaking rules. Unless we went too far we could count on Red as an ally, and often on Mamma also.

Most of the time, however, Mamma stayed neutral, saying neither yes nor no. We seldom pressed her for actual permission to do something. It was enough if she didn't actually forbid it but took refuge in her most used expression: "You know what your papa will say if he finds out." Then Mamma refrained from any further questions, so that she knew nothing in case Papa asked her.

Hayrides were among the most popular forms of amusement for the young folk. A wagon bed was filled with loose hay, and gay couples then drove along country roads while they sang or played games or told jokes, or maybe did a little quiet petting under cover of the darkness.

A hayride never called for planning or a destination. It just began and ended, a gay party on wheels. Sometimes the boys brought along peanuts or candy, sometimes the girls provided cookies or sandwiches. These were consumed as the wagon rolled along, for a picnic supper at night was frowned upon by all adults. Parents expected to be assured that no stops had been made during a hayride, and thus no separating of couples from the crowd. Little did they know, it seemed, how alone a couple can be in the far corner of a load of loose, fragrant hay.

Rusty's birthday fell in mid-August, so we decided on a hayride to celebrate. We wouldn't have to ask Papa's consent, for he was holding a protracted meeting in the country, returning home only on Saturday to be present for his Sunday-morning service. Our ride would be on a Friday night, and Red would use Papa's wagon and mules, left in his charge because he and Papa and Rusty had made a crop that year on fifteen acres of leased land.

The boys, it was agreed, would pool their resources and supply candy and pop, and the girls would all bring cookies. It seemed the ideal way to have a party that need not be censured by the whole town, as it would be if given at the parsonage.

Mamma, when approached with the idea, maintained her neutrality. "It's all right with me, but I'm not sure what your papa would say."

After a consultation, we decided not to risk what Papa might say. So we pledged each couple invited to strict secrecy, sure that ignorance in this case would contribute to Papa's happiness and peace of mind.

Imagine our feelings, then, when the Sunday before our planned celebration Papa based his sermon on sinful pleasures of the world and dwelt at length on the evils that could arise from a hayride! So forceful was his argument against this form of entertainment that he almost had us feeling that the Devil had invented hay, just as a temptation for mankind.

How had he found out? Anxiously we waited for the showdown with Papa, but to our surprise he left again for his country mission without making any reference to our plans. Greatly relieved, we decided the sermon had been pure coincidence, so we went joyfully ahead, convinced that Papa need never know.

Except for the fact that it had rained for two days previously, it was an ideal night for a hayride. We had clear sky, a pale moon that didn't give too much light, and hay so freshly cut its fragrance was intoxicating. In the summer before, Rusty had acquired a guitar, on which he had learned to pick chords, and his repertoire of ballads guaranteed entertainment.

All went delightfully well until Red struck a mudhole about five miles from town. Water from the recent rains had turned a low place in the road into a morass that appeared to have no bottom. The more the mules strained and pulled, the deeper the wagon wheels settled. When the exhausted mules finally gave up, so did Red. Rolling up his pants legs as high as they would go, he nobly waded in and carried the girls to safety, refusing all offers of help from the other boys. Perhaps he felt to blame; perhaps he figured that in numbers lay safety. Surely no scandal would grow out of a deed of valor when eight girls were rescued with absolute impartiality.

Efforts of the boys to extricate the wagon were abandoned around midnight, and we started the long walk home, arriving in the small hours of the morning, footsore and weary.

Needless to say, Papa learned about that hayride! Eight indignant mothers reported separately to him not only that her daughter had been kept out till the disgraceful hour of 2:00 A.M. but that Red had subjected her to improper manhandling. He also heard about it from several of his deacons, who felt strongly that Papa's children should practice what he preached, and from the farmer who had to help Red free his stuck wagon the next day. Utterly crushed with humiliation, Papa appealed to us in a body.

"How do you think I feel, having just preached on the sin of such things, to find my own children took my own wagon . . ."

Words failed him at that point, and he appealed to Mamma. "Easter, what can I do when my own family doesn't listen to my preaching?"

Mamma wasn't very sympathetic. "Try preaching *for* something instead of against so many things."

Papa preached against card-playing so vigorously that we weren't even allowed a deck of flinch cards, then the vogue for those who felt there was contamination in the very touch of what were known as "gambling cards." Cards were cards to Papa, who wouldn't have known a spade from a diamond, and because he felt no need of amusing himself he did not understand why others should.

For weeks I suspected that Mamma knew about the borrowed flinch cards with which Rusty and I played in the secrecy of his room. I was sure of it the night she said, as I started in to "study" with Rusty, "If I hear you two fighting in there over those lessons, I'm going to burn those cards, I don't care who they belong to."

The cards belonged to Billy Blake, and Rusty had such respect for Mamma's threat that for several nights he didn't cheat and we had a peaceable game. Then one night he grew careless and I caught him, and before the smoke of battle had cleared away the cards were in the firebox of the kitchen range. When Rusty asked how he could explain to Billy, Mamma told him he could spend all his after-school hours for the next two weeks cleaning and whitewashing the barn and chicken house and she'd buy Billy a new flinch game. But it would not be brought back again into the parsonage. "It stops being a game when you get mad about it," she said firmly.

Papa preached against shows of any kind, certain they were all snares laid by the Tempter. Mamma, more broad-minded, sometimes took a stand that distressed and embarrassed Papa. Such was the time she consented to my taking a part in a home-talent play put on by the schoolteachers to raise money for the poor at Christmas. The play was called *The Old Maids' Convention,* and perhaps the reason Mamma sent me into the seventh heaven of delight by permitting me to take part was that I played the pickaninny, thoroughly disguised by burned cork. And I always felt the reason my acting career was so short-lived was Papa's prayer that night that I might not be snared into such a life of sin.

Soon after we moved to the Territory, rumors reached us that a machine had been invented that could make pictures move, bringing figures on a screen to life. Mamma, a progressive soul at heart, was extremely interested, even though a little skeptical. When it was announced that these "flickers" would be brought for a one-night stand to our local opera house, a long room over a hardware store reached by an outside stairway, Mamma announced her intention of going. Papa's protests failed to change her mind.

"I won't believe it until I see it for myself. How can a person learn if they don't go see new things?"

Papa said sternly, "Don't you know those must have been the very words Eve used to tempt Adam to disobey God?"

Mamma's conscience appeared undisturbed. "But Adam was weak or he wouldn't have listened. I know you won't be tempted to go, so you can keep the girls and let Ennen and the boys go with me."

Papa groaned. "With my own family there, what can I say about it?"

"Wait till I come home and I'll tell you," Mamma said.

So on the night of the first cinema show in the Indian Territory, four enraptured sinners watched a miracle unfold before their eyes. Even Papa could not have disapproved of that moving picture of an old maid preparing for her first beau, for it never got her away from the mirror before which she worked

204

on her face and hair. And the performance was too awe-inspiring to tempt the imagination to conjecture about what might happen after the man arrived.

Mamma's report to Papa was given with enthusiasm.

"Jim, I know you'll find this hard to believe, but we saw it with our own eyes. She actually powdered her face and combed her hair and pulled up her stocking——"

Too late, she saw that her enthusiasm had run away with her judgment. Papa's face registered shock as he lost sight of the marvels of science and remembered only that our morals had been endangered by Mamma's worldliness.

"Easter, how could you sit there and watch such a thing with your own sons beside you! I simply don't know what the world is coming to."

Mamma, who had laughed harder during that flicker than I'd ever seen her do, said thoughtfully, "I believe it's coming to a new and wonderful age."

Even when most rebellious against Papa's social restrictions, I always sensed that he lacked only understanding, never the qualities of mercy and kindness. Papa was a saint, and saints did not have the temptations of ordinary mortals, nor were their needs the same. Because he found his ascetic interests wholly satisfying, he never doubted their power to satisfy others. He joyfully shared his world with us and was completely bewildered when it didn't seem to supplant wordly things.

On the whole, we were a happy family group at the parsonage, and the times we had to join forces against Papa and his ally, God, only strengthened the ties between us. If our loyalty was sometimes misplaced, at least it tried to give the service of love.

Often my loyalties were so divided between Rusty on the one hand, and the church and school against which he was in constant rebellion on the other, that the strain was severe. Always on the defensive for him, I would often fib without any provocation, calling down his wrath instead of his gratitude. Many times I turned in schoolwork with his name on it because he appeared utterly indifferent to a lesson assignment, only to realize later that my understanding of the subject was far inferior to Rusty's and that I had won for him demerits he might not have had except for my ill-timed intervention. At such times we both shared in the ignominious results, at school as well as at home.

One pleasure all the sinners shared was music. Many of our evenings were spent gathered about the reed organ, singing hymns and such old favorites as "Annie Laurie" and "Old Black Joe." After Rusty got his guitar and Red had sent to Sears Roebuck for a banjo on which he painstakingly learned to pick simple tunes, we began to envision a musical career for all of us. We also had a family vocal quartet, with Winnie Harper carrying the soprano part, and we were quite ready to vocalize for church or B.Y.P.U. at the slightest encouragement.

The B.Y.P.U. was a church-sponsored young people's union, which I always suspected had been thought up solely to prevent our joining the groups who found more pleasure in hiking and Kodaking and buggy-riding on Sunday afternoons. Until the sinners went into action the young people's union was having a hard time competing with outdoor attractions. But after we put our heads together and planned some features to add to our programs, there was a noticeable decline of interest in Sunday-afternoon Kodaking.

Papa was greatly pleased with the increased attendance and the interest being shown by young people from the other churches, and he made frequent reference to "the devotion and loyalty of our young Christians." The adult members rarely attended any of our meetings, so it was something of a shock to glance out of the church window one Sunday afternoon just in time to catch a glimpse of Papa's tall figure headed toward the door. Red caught my frantic signal and stopped his banjo-playing, but Rusty, intent on his guitar, kept right on singing and strumming, blissfully unaware that Papa and the Methodist minister stood in the doorway listening to the slightly risqué song about an old maid who caught a burglar under her bed.

The next Sunday our program was confined to mission posts in China, with an adult sponsor looking on. And before long Papa was wondering why the B.Y.P.U. was not showing the healthy growth it had for a while.

Papa also found it difficult to understand the boys' taste in literature. After he caught Rusty reading a Nick Carter book while kneeling before his chair during family altar, he confiscated the offending paperbacks and forbade any more such "trash" being brought into the house.

It was several weeks later that Mamma took one of her periodic debugging orgies, which meant that every bed in the house had to be dismantled and the corners of the mattresses and the crevices of the wooden bedsteads painted by a feather dipped in a formaldehyde solution to make sure no wily bedbug had escaped her vigilance.

Neither of the boys was at home that Saturday morning, and when Mamma asked Papa to help me with their bed I was thrown into a panic. Only the week before, while putting on clean sheets, I had discovered Rusty's hidden treasure of Nick Carters between the mattresses.

Flying into their room only a minute ahead of Papa, I just had time to lift the mattress and snatch up the forbidden books, then look about wildly for a safer hiding place. None presented itself, and there wasn't time to think. Dashing on into Papa's study, I ran up the roll top of his desk, dropped the books inside, and pulled down the top again. Mamma would keep Papa busy all morning, and I'd soon get a chance to return Rusty's books to where he would expect to find them.

Before the room was finished, a wedding party arrived and everything else was forgotten. Papa always had to be hurried when a couple were waiting, clean clothes found and put in his hand. Dutch had to be coaxed to keep Pugsy and Dodo in the kitchen, for Dutch adored weddings and never missed one if she could help it. Then my hands had to be washed and my hair smoothed, because a witness was needed and Mamma smelled too strongly of formaldehyde.

By the time it was all over, Mamma had finished the boys' bed and I forgot the books that hadn't been replaced.

Late that same day a field worker from the Baptist Home Mission Board arrived to stay over Sunday. Imagine Papa's embarrassed chagrin when he opened his desk under the critical eyes of his guest!

Within a few days the report was all over town that Parson Reaves read Nick Carter books behind the cover of his Bible. When Papa was questioned about it he refused any comment, which meant he was also questioned by Mamma.

"Why don't you just tell them the truth?"

Papa looked from my guilt-stricken face to Rusty's red one, then reproachfully at Red, who was entirely innocent.

"I'd just as soon they'd think I read such things as to know my children couldn't be trusted."

No one replied to that, but a little later Rusty came to the kitchen with his cherished books, thrusting them one by one into the stove.

25

The parlor of the parsonage, known to us as the "marriage room," was almost sacred. The rest of the house might be in a state of disorder, but never the marriage room. It had to be kept ready for use without an instant's warning. It also represented a small source of income not to be discounted.

If there was a lack of money to meet some critical need, we always found encouragement in the thought that there was a good possibility of a wedding. A decision to marry by people we had never heard of could mean a stroke of luck for the sinners. Quite often a long drive had to be made to obtain the license, and so the girl came along to save another trip. More often than not they came to the parsonage, for Papa's popularity as "the marrying parson" had spread abroad.

A marriage fee, though small, could mean meat several times for the table, new or mended shoes for one of us, or the means of meeting any number of family emergencies. Out of every dollar Papa received for marrying a couple, ninety cents went to Mamma, ten cents to the church. What went to Mamma went to all of us, and we became so wedding-conscious that we were able to estimate at a glance the potential fee a couple represented.

But such an estimate was never based on the quality of their clothing or the rig the man drove. Sometimes the ones with kid gloves and high-stepping horses added only a dollar or less to the family funds. The two-dollar-and-up weddings were indicated by the light in the young man's eyes or the width of his grin or the impatience with which he waited for Papa to make them one.

Papa never had a set fee for marriage ceremonies. When a new bridegroom took him aside to ask how much he owed him, Papa's reply was always the same, accompanied by a warm smile that came straight from his heart: "Whatever you feel she is worth to you."

This reply, given utterly without guile, often put an ardent lover on the spot and resulted in a bigger fee than the man might have anticipated. There were occasional five-dollar weddings, a rare ten-dollar one, but the average estimate a groom put upon his bride was two dollars.

Whether he paid little or much or nothing at all, as was sometimes the case, Papa gave each bridegroom the same smiling advice: "Keep on courting her and your marriage will stand the test. A woman likes to hear you say you love her."

Occasionally our judgment erred in estimating the pay dirt Papa might strike. Once Dutch, watching from the window as a well-dressed middle-aged man tenderly assisted a plump woman from a rig drawn by two matched horses, called excitedly to Papa, "Hurry up and get ready, Papa. Here comes a five-dollar wedding."

She proved to be way off. After the vows were said, the man drew Papa aside to say that he had no money with him but would bring Papa a nice fee the first time he came to town. "She's got a good farm and money in the bank, but you can see I couldn't ask her for any just yet."

Another time we missed an estimate was when I tried to

hurry Papa, who had been caught working in the garden minus the white collar and tie without which he did not consider he had properly and legally tied a knot.

"Don't bother, Papa. It's likely just a free wedding, anyway. They haven't spoken all the time they've been waiting."

That day I served as one of the two witnesses required by law, as I often did when couples came to the parsonage without the sufficient number of relatives or friends. Watching the nervous groom, I thought he was surely the most unhappy one I had ever seen, and the bride quite the homeliest. No new shoes for Dutch as we had hoped!

But when the man asked the usual question and Papa gave his smiling "Just whatever you feel she is worth to you" reply, the groom put back into his worn wallet the dollar he had started to take out, then handed Papa a ten-dollar bill. "I wish it was more," he said apologetically. "She's worth a lot to me."

Papa, who loved people, was never happier than when he was officiating at a wedding. He often crawled uncomplainingly out of bed, and once, I remember, he answered a midnight call to go across town to marry a young woman who did not belong to his church. It was a cold, snowy night, and Papa decided he would rather walk the dozen blocks than have his horse waiting in the cold.

When he returned home, chilled to the bone and with wet feet, Mamma scolded as she got up to heat a sadiron to put into the bed.

"It does look like they would have brought you home. How much did they give you for going over there at this unearthly hour, anyway?"

"Nothing," Papa admitted. "It was Mr. Simms' sister getting married and he held a shotgun on the man. How could I expect a groom to pay for that kind of ceremony?"

Another shotgun wedding Papa had was when the bridegroom carried the gun. And Papa didn't get paid for this one either.

A church member came to ask him to help dissuade her sister from marrying a half-breed Indian who had the reputation of being a man of violent temper and dangerous if crossed. The woman feared for her sister's happiness unless she got over her infatuation for the man.

Always ready to be helpful, Papa went to see the young woman, a vivacious and beautiful blonde, and patiently reminded her of the sacred obligations of marriage and how necessary mutual respect was in such a relationship. She tearfully agreed that perhaps she should break her engagement.

The next night the Indian appeared at our house with a rifle in his hands, looking as ferocious as one of his ancestors on the warpath. "Come with me," he told Papa. "Either you'll marry me or I'll kill you."

Mamma, protesting, was waved back by a threatening gesture with the rifle. "Let him come," she was warned. "He told her not to marry me, now he will tell her to do it." He took out a paper, which he waved triumphantly. "I've got the license, too."

Papa, not looking nearly as upset as the rest of us, took his hat and left with his armed escort. Mamma laughed a little shakily and told us not to worry. "He doesn't want to kill Papa. He just wants to get married."

An hour later Papa was back, looking as undisturbed as though it was nothing unusual to have armed men appear at the door. "Well?" Mamma asked. "Did you marry them?"

Papa shook his head. "I had prayer first, and while I was praying her brother-in-law grabbed the gun and called the marshal. He's in jail, but I think in the morning I'll go down and try to get him out. I don't think he's so bad. I think he was just bluffing."

But before Papa was ready for bed the pretty blonde came to the parsonage, her face streaked with tears. "Oh, Brother Reaves, I can't stand having him in that jail. Please go get him out and marry us. I'll promise you he'll never make trouble for you again if you will."

"Trouble for me, Sister Helen? I'm not worrying about myself. But what about trouble for you if you marry a man like this, of whom your family disapproves?"

She looked at him wide-eyed. "What does it matter if he makes trouble for me, Brother Reaves? I love him."

Papa sighed and reached for his hat. "Then there's no use waiting."

It was two hours before Papa returned, and Mamma never said anything about us going to bed. How could we be expected to sleep with Papa at the mercy of that angry gunman?

But when the two men came, it was Papa who carried the rifle. Indian Joe, looking very subdued, spoke sheepishly to the red-eyed Helen.

"It's all right, he says he will marry us. He's our friend. We'll just stay here tonight."

I thought Papa looked startled, but Mamma was too angry to notice. "Well, get that gun out of here," she said. "This may be a hotel but it's not a battleground."

At that moment there was a pounding on the door, and in a flash the Indian was back to type. Snatching the gun from Papa, he backed against the wall, rifle barrel aimed on the door. Mamma, looking scared, pushed us all into the farthest corner of the room as Papa went to open the door.

It was Helen's angry brother-in-law, followed by her weeping sister. "Brother Reaves," the man stormed, "the marshal says you got that crazy Indian out of jail and promised to marry him to Helen. If you do, you're through in this town. I'll run you out if it's the last thing I ever do."

He saw the rifle in Indian Joe's hands then and stopped, his beet-red face turning chalky white. Indian Joe said softly, "He's going to marry us because he's my friend. And because I kill you if he don't."

Papa started to remonstrate with Joe, but he repeated, his very calmness a terrifying thing, "You marry us quick or I'll kill him."

"Do it!" the sister screamed. "Go ahead, Brother Reaves."

But Papa looked at her husband.

"Shall I take a chance and refuse?"

"Go ahead," the man gasped. "You can't take a chance on a wild Indian with a gun. Helen will just have to make the best of it."

So, with plenty of witnesses that time, Papa said the words that made the swarthy Indian and the blonde Helen man and wife, pretending to be unaware of the rifle the bridegroom held in one arm. His prayer was a little shorter than usual, however, and the instant it was over Papa reached for the rifle. Joe relinquished it, beaming at his bride.

"Everything is fine now. Nobody will get killed."

The relatives took a hasty departure, after assuring Joe they bore him no ill will. Mamma, however, had not surrendered. "Get that thing out of my house," she ordered. "We've had enough gun play for one night."

Papa was grinning broadly. "It's harmless, Easter. A rifle won't shoot without a cartridge in it." Reaching into his coat pocket, he drew out three shells. "You see, Joe and I agreed it might be safer if it wasn't loaded."

Joe's smile matched Papa's. "The parson is my friend. He has made me a married man and a good citizen."

Mamma was silent a moment, then she began to smile. "Well, friends, I think it's time we were all getting to bed if you're sure the battle is over."

214

After the house was dark and quiet I heard Mamma say to Papa in the bed across the room, "Just the same, Jim Reaves, don't get the idea you can start inviting all the couples you marry to bed down here afterward."

"I didn't invite him to stay," Papa answered. "I just told him we were his friends and he took it for granted that he'd be welcome."

Mamma sighed, but it didn't sound as if she were much upset. "Maybe he was right. Now for pity's sake let's get to sleep. I'll need to get up early to cook them a nice wedding breakfast."

The story of that wedding spread over the town like wildfire, and Papa received so much criticism that Rusty had several fights the following week, though most of his friends remained stanchly loyal in saying that Papa had a right to be afraid of Indian Joe's gun.

But what even these friends couldn't understand was Papa's close friendship with Joe, which grew through the years in spite of the fact that the gun-toting Indian quickly abandoned his role of good citizen. Papa never wanted the true story of that shotgun wedding told, for he didn't want Helen's brother-in-law to feel he had been duped. It was enough for Papa that peace had been declared.

Papa married many runaway couples, yet he would just as quickly refuse to perform such a hurried ceremony. More than once he prayed over a young couple until they agreed to go home and weigh their decision. Several times he insisted upon accompanying them to their homes to win their parents' consent.

Once he gave me the thrill of aiding a couple escape from their angry pursuers. I kept the relatives waiting for a half-hour while I pretended to be searching for Papa, who was then driving the newlyweds to the depot to catch a train just due. He could do this with a clear conscience, for the bridegroom was sixty-five, his bride fifty-seven. Her children objected violently to the marriage, claiming the man's only interest was in the widow's farm. Her son threatened to beat up Papa when he learned they'd been tricked, but Papa just beamed and invited them all to stay for dinner. Since it was well past noon by then and they faced a ten-mile drive back to the farm, they simmered down and accepted.

No one could hurry Papa about preparing for a wedding. Many a nervous bridegroom fidgeted as he waited for the minister to appear, often asking me why he was taking so long. I never knew what to say, even though I knew the answer. An impatient bridegroom could not be expected to understand that Papa did not feel worthy to marry him until he had shaved, had put on his best clothes and a fresh wing collar and bow tie, and had taken time to pray about what he was asked to do.

One time a couple came to him who were obviously under the legal age they had given for the record. Papa looked from the license they had presented to the frightened face of the girl and asked kindly, "Honey, how old are you?"

"Eighteen," she faltered, but even I could see she was lying. Papa turned to me. "Go tell your mamma I need her for another witness."

He didn't, really. A witness had only to be able to sign a certificate and old enough to testify to the marriage if necessary. So Mamma had permitted Dutch to go in with me, and neither one of us would like having things changed. But when I repeated Papa's message to Mamma, she took off her apron and smoothed her hair, saying thoughtfully, "I wonder what's bothering him."

Papa came right to the point. "Easter, this child says she's eighteen, but she doesn't look it. Would you say she is old enough to be married?"

Mamma studied the flushed face of the girl for a moment and then said quietly, "Yes, Jim, I would."

Only in matters of church policy did Papa ever question Mamma's judgment. The ceremony was performed, the usual advice offered after the fervent prayer for their happiness, then the newlyweds went their way.

The next day an irate father appeared, ready to take vengeance upon Papa for marrying his daughter. "That girl is only fourteen," he stormed. "Any man with a grain of sense could see that she wasn't of age."

"They had the license," Papa said defensively. "It authorized any minister to perform the ceremony. If I hadn't married them, someone else would have."

That didn't satisfy the angry parent. "All you wanted was your fee," he yelled. "You didn't care what happened to a child without sense enough to know what she was doing. For two cents I'd horsewhip you, preacher or no preacher."

Papa stood up, his great height towering over the other man. "You can try it," he said calmly, "but I doubt if you can do it. And nothing you do or say will undo what's been done. Your daughter is married in the sight of God and two witnesses, and you have to make the best of it."

The man left, apparently not convinced of the wisdom of trying to horsewhip the big preacher. But as soon as he was gone Papa wilted, turning stricken eyes on Mamma. "Fourteen years old, just a child. Easter, what have I done? But you said——"

"I said she looked old enough to be married, and I still say it. Jim, stop blaming yourself. The day will come before too long when that man will be wanting to thank you for marrying that child."

The father, whenever he could find a listener, continued to abuse Papa and make threats about what he was going to do to him, all of which Papa ignored. Then suddenly the threats

217

stopped, and Papa heard through a neighbor of the family that the couple had gone to live with her parents and peace was restored.

Months later the same neighbor stopped Papa one day. "They've got a nine-pound boy over there, Preacher. And I think if that girl's father wasn't ashamed to, he'd come around and thank you for marrying them, seeing it's only been a little over six months."

Papa looked at Mamma curiously that night after he had relayed the news to her. "Could you tell that day, Easter? Was that why you said she was old enough to be married?"

Mamma said enigmatically, "I just knew she was a woman and not a child."

In the thirty-six years that the "marrying parson" served his section of the Indian Territory, he recorded well over five thousand marriages, and it was his happy boast that only one, to his knowledge, ended in divorce. Papa's marriages were really made in heaven.

26

It was easy to see that Papa was greatly worried. His prayers at altar time were so long that I worked four problems in algebra one night and Dutch went to sleep and he never even noticed. He had also failed for a week to pray for Rusty, who had been gone for a month on one of what had come to be periodic hobo trips over the country. School, Rusty had decided, was less educational than life.

Because Papa always brought his troubles to Mamma as well as to God, I overheard enough to know that his halo was slipping a little with his church. Some of the members, it seemed, felt that he was being much too friendly with the ministers of the other churches, now numbering four since the Episcopalians had added enough strength to have a part-time rector. After all, weren't the churches competing with each other in getting members? Then how could Papa, as the leader of one group, fraternize with his competitors?

Yet Papa was warm friends with the Methodist pastor, he preached a funeral service in cooperation with the Christian minister at the request of the relatives of the deceased, and he filled the Presbyterian pulpit one Sunday morning when the pastor became ill and Papa's pulpit was being taken by a visiting clergyman. But topping all his sins, I suspected, was the fact that he permitted me to attend Sunday-afternoon services at the Episcopal Church.

That had started as a bargain with my best friend, Winnie Harper, with whom I had formed one of those loyalty pacts that would not let us be apart if it could possibly be avoided. For two years Winnie had attended all the services of our church, but when the rector of a church in a neighboring town agreed to divide his Sundays with the local Episcopalians, Winnie and I were faced with a problem. The solution we found seemed simple. Papa had agreed that if Winnie continued to attend Sunday school and church with me on Sunday morning and evening, it was only fair that I go with her on Sunday afternoon. The Episcopal service would be over in plenty of time for the B.Y.P.U., which had been moved nearer the night service as something of a compromise with the hiking and Kodak fans.

Papa, I am sure, welcomed a solution of that particular problem, preferring the safety of any church service to the temptations the Devil offered, but many of his members did not agree. They saw no better opportunity for Satan to get in his work than when one was found in the company of misguided believers.

"I just don't understand," Papa said over and over. "I feel I've failed somehow as their pastor to teach them obedience to our Lord's command to love one another."

"Stop blaming yourself," Mamma scolded gently. "The Lord Who gave the commandment was betrayed, remember. If He couldn't force love and understanding, then neither can you. I guess it's something folks have to feel for themselves."

But Papa was not one to quit trying. One spring Sunday he preached a sermon so dynamite-packed that it rocked the whole church. He told his members in simple, earnest words

220

that Christ's love was impartially distributed among all men, saints and sinners alike; that His church, spoken of in the Bible as His bride, included all who loved and trusted Him, no matter how they interpreted his teachings. In short, Papa said flatly that the church Christ founded was composed of all believers in Him, not any one group organized for the purpose of perpetuating certain doctrines.

This, he was quickly told by his deacons, was rank heresy. There was just one true church, which was theirs; only one way to serve God in an acceptable manner—their way, given them by their forefathers. Like Jonadab in the Old Testament, they would not allow their children to be taught any deviation from their faith. Papa was asked to either retract his position or resign. He resigned.

Mamma heartily approved. "What's the use calling yourself a preacher if you need to be told what to preach? We'll manage. Remember what that Home Mission Board worker said about finding you a larger field? It sure would be nice to have a little larger pay."

After spending a night in agonized prayer in his study, Papa came up with an announcement that killed Mamma's short-lived dream of more money. He felt that God wanted him to carry on the work he had begun among isolated rural people. But it was a field not yet opened by the Baptist Home Mission Board, and so he could expect no help from them. His support must come altogether from the people he served.

At this Mamma burst into tears. "Potatoes and fresh pork," she sobbed. "That's all we'll ever get. I simply won't put our children through that kind of life."

"Before you decide about that," Papa said earnestly, "I want you to go with me on a trip into the country. I can show you half-grown children that get enough to eat but have never even been in a schoolhouse or heard the Gospel preached. If we supply them with spiritual food, we can surely trust our Lord to supply material food for ours."

Mamma's reply was typical. "I guess you're right, Jim. And I can find a way to help Him. Maybe Red and I can start a dairy like we had in Waco that first year you were here."

Papa shook his head. "Red must go on to the university like he's planned. The Lord will provide for us."

But he stopped to touch her shoulder gently as he started away. "I'm glad you're willing to help Him, though, Honey. You and Him make a mighty strong combination."

A month later we had moved from the comfortable parsonage into a smaller, unfinished house on a block of land Papa had managed to buy cheaply because it lay across the creek at the edge of town. The walls were unpapered, the floors bare, and the space so limited that the organ had to be put in one end of the long kitchen, which would also serve as a dining room. Yet I think we all echoed Mamma's sentiments when she looked about and said with satisfaction in her voice, "Well, at least it's ours."

Papa and Red were in the midst of building a barn and chicken house and fencing the cowlot when Rusty came home to help, making our happiness complete. Papa bought a shiny new buggy for the family's use and a horse which we named after Dodo.

That horse was young and skittish and hard-mouthed, so that if he decided to run all you could do was hang onto the reins and let him go until he had winded himself. When I was driving I went his way as often as mine, and I learned that this provided an excellent alibi when I didn't want to hurry home. Mamma loathed Dodo so much she wouldn't drive him herself and would believe anything I told her about him.

Life that summer was pleasant, and with chickens and cows and a big garden everyone was busy. But with the re-

straints of a public life removed there was a harmony sometimes lacking in the parsonage. Red and Rusty quit fighting
and made a crop on some rented land. This insured college
for Red in the fall because Rusty, refusing to go back for his
last year in school, generously gave his share of the crop to
Red.

Rusty had found his calling so he was independent. He had
discovered the magic of paint, and it didn't matter to him
where he spread color—on the walls of a house, on a sign
to be nailed on a post or before a building, or beauty put upon
an oilcloth to tack unframed upon our ugly walls. It was all
creative, and it all brought peace to his restless soul. Vaguely
sensing that, I felt a new pride replace all the old tensions
about him.

Papa's preaching often kept him away for weeks at a time,
for roads in the country were almost nonexistent and travel
was measured in time instead of miles. Sometimes he'd get
home several times a week, sometimes once in several weeks.
He drove a team of grays to his light buckboard, and it was
nothing unusual for one of the boys to hear them drive up in
the night and go out to investigate, confident of finding Papa
sound asleep. He had only to turn his horses' heads toward
home, for they knew the way. Those grays were a little like
a leader dog, trained to take care of their master.

Since there were no telephones in the rural areas or any
other means of communication, no one ever knew when Papa
was coming into a neighborhood. He just arrived at a home,
the word spread by way of the grapevine method, and people
gathered, hungry to hear the Gospel but just as hungry for
news of the outside world. He took them what he had to share,
and in return they gave him small offerings of money from
time to time, the potatoes and pork Mamma had anticipated
more often taking the form of vegetables and fruit and meat

in season. And they gave him love and gratitude in place of criticism. So rewarding was this gift that Papa spent over thirty years in the mission field, content to do what no one else wanted to do, to go where no one else bothered to go.

Mamma seldom went with Papa in person, but she was always with him in spirit. Once he told her of a woman he had found living alone in her delapidated farmhouse, refusing to leave the premises or admit anyone. Papa had been asked by neighbors to go talk to her, but she had stopped him with a shotgun before he got within shouting distance. He was greatly concerned about her pitiable plight, having caught a glimpse of her wild, unkempt appearance. Yet, the neighbor-boring farmers told him, she had a good education and had been an alert and attractive woman until the death of her husband some ten years before.

"I think I'll try again," Papa said. "Maybe she'll read a Bible if I take her one."

When he got ready to return to the community Mamma brought out several copies of the *Ladies' Home Journal*. "Take these to your wild woman, Jim. Right now they may do her more good than a Bible."

Papa, who never read anything secular, looked at Mamma reproachfully. "How can you say that? What good can these things do her?"

"They can put her back in touch with the world. That poor woman is just out of step is all. You do as I say, and leave these on her doorstep if she won't let you in."

Papa, though dubious, followed directions. He couldn't get as close as the woman's doorstep, however, so he left the magazines beside the sagging gate. It was several weeks before he went back to that district, and Mamma insisted upon sending two more copies of the magazine. This time the hermitess allowed him to come closer, and she opened her door and snatched up the magazines as he was getting back into his buggy. "They're from my wife," he called out. "She likes to read such things."

Winter kept Papa nearer home, but early in the summer he received word that the men of that isolated area would provide a brush arbor if he would come and hold a meeting.

Driving past the "wild woman's" place his first day in the community, Papa was pleased to see that the sagging gate had been mended, the broken porch repaired, the dirty windows washed and covered with bright curtains.

Wonderingly he stopped and approached the door, still doubtful of his welcome. But it was flung open, and a smiling woman with neat hair and dress called to him. "Come in, mister. I've been hoping you'd stop again. Did you bring me any more of those books?"

It was like seeing the dead brought back to life, Papa reported. "Those magazines started me thinking," she said earnestly. "I guess I'd forgot there was still nice things in the world."

The woman was numbered among Papa's converts that summer, but he gave Mamma the credit. "You and your magazines did it. I never could have reached her."

Mamma looked pleased. "It was just a cup of cold water. But what's better when you're dying of thirst?"

Most of Papa's summer meetings were held under brush arbors. Trees were chopped down and trimmed, then sunk in the ground to form upright supports for a roof made of other trimmed tree trunks, across which was laid a thick layer of leafy branches, providing protection against sun or rain. Backless seats were made by laying rough boards across blocks. To provide comfort and protect against splinters, the women brought heavy quilts to pad the boards. Oil lanterns were hung for lights, and occasionally sawdust was laid in the aisles.

Sometimes a small platform was built for the preacher but as often as not he stood on the ground like the rest.

The second summer after Papa began his evangelistic campaign, he obtained Mamma's consent to load our small organ on the wagon and take me along to play for his meetings. A music-publishing house had sent him a couple of dozen hymnals, so all he needed was an organist.

Winnie Harper and I convinced him that he also needed a song-leader. We weren't exactly moved by altruistic motives, but Papa was the last one to suspect that. With her parents' consent, we became his evangelistic crew during the summer months.

Winnie, a strikingly pretty girl, was a big help in Papa's soul-saving work. Wherever we went, all the farm boys for miles around became greatly interested in their spiritual welfare. If Papa took for granted that it was due to his exhortations, who was to disillusion him? The attention we two young evangelists received that summer proved so flattering that we quite understood why Papa would choose to make soul-saving a life work.

Like his Christ, Papa went about doing good wherever he saw opportunity. Sometimes his preaching took the form of a prayer said over a sick child, a funeral service he might drive forty miles or more to conduct, a marriage performed, or a Bible left in a home. Wherever he went he was welcomed, for he carried the gospel of love in his heart. Often he accepted a challenge that would have discouraged a less consecrated man. Some of his adventures were told so often they became legendary among his people, just as was the tall preacher with his weather-stained black hat, shabby clothes, and wide grin.

One of his mission posts lay across a treacherous river famed for quicksands that made fording dangerous. There were legends of whole herds of cattle disappearing in the river, of men who started across and were never seen again, of narrow escapes of various sorts. The only bridge spanning the stream was almost thirty miles above the one-room schoolhouse where Papa went to preach one Sunday a month.

To cut distance, Papa unhitched his team and left them hobbled, then waded across the river and finished the trip, a distance of about a mile, on foot. His weight was less liable to cause trouble in the sand than that of a horse. Since the water seldom reached above his hips it was a simple matter to disrobe, roll his shoes and clothes into a bundle, and carry them high and dry on his shoulders.

One Sunday morning the river was a little high and running swift. In the middle of the stream Papa stepped into a hole, lost his balance, and almost fell. Instinctively he threw out his hands, allowing his clothes to drop off his shoulder. In the swift current they quickly disappeared, and poor Papa stood clothed in only his hat, twenty miles from home.

It was a drastic situation and one that definitely called for prayer. Obviously he couldn't fill his appointment, and it was equally impossible to recross and drive home in broad daylight in his condition.

In the middle of his prayer, he related, he remembered a farmer living about halfway to the schoolhouse who was an avowed agnostic and had steadfastly refused to go hear Papa preach, though the other members of his family never missed a service. That meant the farmer should be at home, and alone. Papa headed that way, hugging the bushes as he went.

The man ran for his shotgun when Papa appeared in his birthday suit, but after recognizing the visitor and hearing of his predicament, he laughed heartily and produced some clothes of his own that proved to be several sizes too small. "But at least they cover you," he laughed. "And you can drive home barefoot. I'll let folks at the schoolhouse know you're not coming today."

"Oh, but I am," Papa said. "Just as fast as I can get there."

His benefactor stopped laughing to stare at him. "You mean you'll preach looking like that?"

Papa looked down at his muddy bare feet, the ludicrously short trousers, and shirt sleeves that stopped halfway to his elbows, and said, grinning, "I don't imagine that first Baptist preacher looked much fancier in his shirt of camel's hair. Of course I'm preaching. I said I would. Do you have a horse you'll lend me?"

The farmer was laughing again. "I'll drive you over there. I wouldn't miss this for anything."

En route to the schoolhouse the scorner attempted to rib Papa a little. "What would you have done if I hadn't been home this morning, preacher? Maybe this God you pray to kept me away from the meeting to help you out."

"Maybe He did," Papa answered gravely. "And then maybe He took my clothes away from me so I would come and take you to church. He's more interested in your soul than how I look."

Papa literally went into the highways and hedges, and sometimes he even compelled the people to come in. Such was the time a woman appealed to him because her husband refused the family permission to attend the brush-arbor meeting Papa was holding. "My children have never heard a sermon, living in these backwoods like we do," she enlisted Papa's sympathy by saying. "Maybe if you'd talk to him he'd take us."

Papa found the man working in his field and very unwilling to discuss the matter. When Papa insisted upon doing so the man advanced upon him, hoe upraised threateningly. "Get off my land before I chop your fool head off," he yelled.

Standing his ground, Papa said quietly, "It's not your land.

228

It belongs to God, like everything else in the world. Like my head. So go ahead, chop off God's head if you want to. But I'm not leaving till you listen to me."

Throwing down the hoe, the farmer took a belligerent stance with his fists. "If you wasn't wearing that swallowtail coat I'd mop up the ground with you."

Papa, who hated violence of any kind, began to take off the coat. "I'll let you try to do it, provided you promise to take your family to church tonight if you fail."

It must have been a history-making battle, to judge by Papa's face when he got home a week later. It ended in victory for the preacher, who had the advantage of size if not skill. Sitting on his prostrate victim to hold him down, Papa prayed aloud till the man surrendered.

The family came to the meeting that night and each night after that until Papa left, when the man put several bushels of potatoes into the preacher's buggy. "I guess they're God's taters since they growed on His land," he said, grinning. "Thanks, Preacher, for straightening me out."

27

Statehood brought many exciting changes, but none equaled the stirring days of the fight over the county seat. The new state constitution provided that an election could be called to relocate a county seat should the voters so petition. Two other towns challenged ours, making it a three-way fight. Interest was at fever heat, and anyone of any age who did not take up arms was branded as a traitor.

Even Papa abandoned his role of missionary for that of politician, convinced that the best interests of the people would be served by leaving the seat of local government where it had been placed by the constitutional convention.

Papa's loyalty was also challenged by the stories being put out, saying our town was not a safe place to build a new court-house because of the danger of floods, and by personal attacks made upon the business leaders of our community, who were being branded as unfriendly and unfair in their dealings.

The campaign lasted all summer, with the election held in late fall. It was an irony of fate that it should be one of the rainiest seasons we had ever known. The back roads, barely passable in good weather, turned into quagmires that kept active campaigning confined to places that could be reached by train.

Undaunted, Papa went into isolated communities under difficulties that would have stopped anyone with less zeal. Most of the men among whom he campaigned had never voted, because the privilege had been denied them as settlers in the Indian Territory. Papa believed they needed to be aroused to this new responsibility, and so cold rains and mud didn't stop him, though he spent many a night sleeping on his buggy seat while hopelessly mired down in oozy clay.

Prominent speakers from surrounding states were brought in to join in the county-seat fight. Among them was a federal judge who was scheduled to attend a rally at a distant point in the county. Papa was appointed to see that he got there, since the rally was in an inland town.

It had stopped raining but the world was a sea of mud the day the judge arrived by train, aware that the rest of his journey must be made by horse and rig. He was a fastidiously dressed man who looked askance at the muddy streets and suggested they forego the drive into the country. Papa, afraid he was about to lose an ace speaker, made a rash promise. "I'll promise you won't even get your feet muddy."

Even though Papa had allowed plenty of time for the trip, they arrived two hours late and the eminent jurist was the last speaker introduced. He made his talk brief but convincing.

"I've learned a lot on the trip here, both about the caliber of the men in your county and your need for roads. All I can say about this election fight is that if a man like Mr. Reaves, who carried me on his back for a half-mile today to keep his promise not to let my feet get muddy, wants the county seat kept in his town, then I think it ought to stay there."

It was in late summer that the thing feared most by our town happened. The creek, swollen by weeks of rain and unable to empty into the full river, went out of its banks. Though the whole town was not flooded, the threat was present and the quarter-mile-wide stream presented a most fearful appearance. All approaches to town from our side were cut off, and Red, Rusty, and I spent the most of the day at the creek, watching the rising water and occasionally rescuing pigs or chickens washed downstream.

Rusty hurriedly made a scow out of a big hogtrough, and in this we paddled along the water's edge, careful not to get in the swift current of midstream. Papa was away, but news of the flood, we knew, would hurry him back, since he did not have to cross the creek in order to get home.

Shortly after noon a wagon drove up, and two men jumped out and unloaded a boat. They also had a camera, and Red soon learned that they were newspaper men from the town making the strongest bid to take the courthouse away from us.

"It's in the bag now," they said gleefully. "Just wait till we get pictures of Main Street under water. Nobody but a fool will vote to build a courthouse here then."

"You try to cross that current and you might see a few sights you don't like," Red warned them. "That water's swift, and there's submerged barb-wire fences you can't see. It's dangerous to try to get into town now."

His warning was frankly distrusted. "Oh, yeah? Look, fellow, you can't scare us off that easy. We're rowing our boat right down Main Street, and we're taking a picture of the lake where you folks proposed to have the taxpayers build a courthouse."

"Okay, go ahead," Red said good-naturedly. "But if you get into trouble, don't expect any help."

We watched while the men launched their boat and took off. Less than halfway across they were caught in the roiling current, whirled about, and slammed into a tree. The boat overturned, but the men managed to scramble to safety in the tree.

Their shouts for help could be plainly heard, but they were met with derisive laughter from all of us gathered at the water's edge. "You wanted to look at the water!" we took turns yelling at them. "Stay there and take a good look."

Attracted by the yells, all the residents of the South Side came to hoot at the marooned enemy and make derisive jeers. When night came they still clung to their precarious perch, either unable to swim or afraid to attempt it in the treacherous water. A fine, cold mist began, and we went home, still hilarious over the plight of the enemy. But when Papa arrived home, shortly after dark, he didn't see anything funny in the situation.

"Do you mean you haven't tried to help them? Why, it's cold enough to give them pneumonia. I'm ashamed of you boys."

"But, Papa, we told you they were from Elwood and came to take pictures——"

"I don't care if they are from Hades and Satan himself. It's inhuman to leave them in that tree all night. Have you any kind of boat I can use?"

"It's not really a boat," Rusty hastened to say. "It would swamp with you, Papa."

Papa just stood there, looking from one to the other. "Well?"

Red sighed and got up. "Oh, all right. Rusty and me will go."

Mamma made a quick protest. "Jim, it's dangerous. They can both drown if they run into wire in the dark."

"I know," Papa said soberly. "But leaving your neighbor in the ditch and passing by on the other side is more dangerous. Suppose one or both of those men get so cold they fall off that tree tonight? Do you think the boys would ever have any self-respect again?"

The rescue was made, with Papa's shouts and a lighted

233

lantern to guide the boys in their makeshift boat back to safety. It took two trips, and they were all wet and shivering when they got back to the house.

After a warm supper the men were given the boys' bed, leaving my brothers to sleep on the kitchen floor. Early the next morning the men left, after profuse expressions of gratitude.

The next week we received a copy of the Elwood *Express* in the mail, with a marked editorial. In that the story of the rescue was told, making Red and Rusty heroes. "With youth like these our new state need not be afraid of its future, whether or not mistakes are made in locating public buildings. Our true strength lies in homes where love and kindness are taught and the enemy is not turned away hungry."

Both boys had red faces as they finished reading. Rusty said in a funny, shame-filled voice, "Do you suppose he knew Papa had to make us go?"

Red was then twenty-two and Rusty almost twenty, but they were just boys to Papa. He never let his children grow up, insofar as his own judgement of them went. At seventeen I had to slip out on dates, for Papa did not think a girl should permit a boy to pay her attention unless she were seriously interested in him. And certainly he didn't think I should be serious at that age. Papa just didn't understand the appeal of fun, or the fact that the forbidden fruit is always sweetest.

He would have been shocked if he had seen me riding horseback the next morning after the rescue, together with two neighbor girls, for as soon as we were out of sight of the house we got astride, though we were not wearing riding skirts. That meant a bold exposure of lower limbs such as nice girls didn't permit themselves. But we did not expect to meet anyone, as we had chosen a little-used country road leading past the old Indian cemetery.

I was riding Dodo, the hard-mouth, and he jogged along quietly enough until a man came riding toward us. The other girls instantly changed into a more ladylike position, but as I started to follow suit a piece of paper blew against Dodo's leg.

He shied violently, throwing us against the barbed-wire fence around the cemetery. Caught completely off balance, I fell over the fence, but a foot was caught in the stirrup. Dodo bolted, dragging me through six strands of wire and down the road, until the man we had seen stopped him and picked up what was left of me. I felt as if most of myself had been left clinging to those wire barbs along with scraps of my clothing.

Mamma seldom lost her head, but she was thrown into utter confusion about what to do with my remnants, since getting the doctor appeared to be out of the question. She did finally reach him on the telephone, and he gave detailed instructions about sticking my almost severed ear back on and making other repairs. In the midst of these lengthy directions the doctor said, "Hold on, here's Rusty. If he can make it across the creek, so can I."

Rusty had taken one look at me and made for the hog-trough boat. A half-hour later he triumphantly escorted in the brave doctor, who unzipped my ear and set it on a little more symmetrically and put me back together in miraculous fashion. He stayed with us two days until the creek was down, not feeling equal to another hair-raising trip in that hogtrough with Rusty.

Papa was at a loss to understand how the accident could have happened. "I thought you could sit on a horse," he kept saying, and I preferred being considered dumb than to have him know how brash I had been.

The art of deception had developed in me by then until

I led something like a Jekyll-and-Hyde life insofar as Papa was concerned. It seemed so much simpler than argument, so much kinder than disillusionment.

So Papa never knew that while he was preaching on the evils of picture shows, then becoming very popular, I was playing the piano in the orchestra pit of our movie house every Friday night, while Winnie feelingly sang a popular song which was illustrated on the screen. We had found this the ideal way to get into the show without paying. Since the spotlights were always on Winnie, never on the pianist, I felt little fear of discovery.

Papa never knew, either, about the Sunday-afternoon buggy rides until he found out quite by accident. The young man and I were a couple of miles from home, guiding the livery rig along a wooded road, when we met another buggy at such a narrow place that it was necessary for one of us to turn out and stop. I was horrified to see that the driver of the other buggy was Papa, returning from a Sunday preaching mission. And I was heading away from home, and I was holding the reins myself when Papa met us, with the young man's arm across the back of the seat! That poor fellow almost had to marry me. It was hard for Papa to believe that I had not compromised my virtue.

Papa approved of the Literarys held at the country school-houses, where recitations and singing were offered for entertainment. But he never knew how much fun they were after the older people and the children had gone home and the dancing began. Nor did he know how a box supper, planned to raise money for some worthy cause, offered opportunity for flirtation and excitement. So much that Papa knew, and so much that he didn't.

One thing he was strict about when he was home was a ten-o'clock curfew. He went to bed very early, but he had an uncanny habit of waking promptly at ten, then getting up to see if I was safely in bed. If I wasn't, the procedure was always the same. Papa dressed, took his lantern, and started out to look for me.

Betrayed by the bobbing lantern, he never found me, of course. There was always a quiet way around a moving object, and by the time Papa gave up and came back to the house I was sleeping as peacefully as Dutch. And he couldn't prove I hadn't just been at the outhouse when he'd first looked.

The humiliation of having my escorts witness this lack of trust in me seared my very soul, especially if it were a first date and the boy never asked for a second. Then I pitied myself most thoroughly.

One morning Papa found a new straw sailor in the orchard, behind a chicken-wire fence. It hadn't been there the day before. Had my date and I been in the orchard, of all places?

This had serious aspects, and the truth fell a good deal short of satisfying Papa. He saw no logical reason why a youth, if innocent, should bolt and run when he saw that bobbing lantern coming toward him, or why he'd keep running after the wind had caught and sailed his hat over the high fence. Again we almost had a shotgun wedding, though the youth never knew about his narrow escape.

Papa, it often seemed to me, trusted everyone and everything to God—but me.

Epilogue

On a night in February, 1935, the wind howled mournfully around the big concrete house that was so oddly reminiscent of its builder—three stories high, with a slightly gangling look, and yet suggesting strength and dependability. People who knew "Old Parson Reaves" always smiled at sight of that house. He had made every cement block in it with his own hands, working in his spare hours over a period of years. It looked like him.

The house appeared older that it was. It had been standing among the big oak trees for less than a quarter of a century, but it looked as though it had grown there, its weather-beaten roof and gables and gray walls completely covered with English ivy. We sometimes called the big house Noah's Ark, for it had so often provided a refuge for us in times of sickness or childbirth or hard luck. When some of us had remonstrated with Papa about building such a large house after half the children were married and the others nearly grown, our parents had just smiled at each other as Mamma said serenely, "It'll be roomy enough that any of you can come back when you want to."

So the new house quickly became home to even those sinners who were already married and had homes of their own. We went back for family reunions at Thanksgiving or Christmas, or for anniversary celebrations, or for no reason at all. And Mamma put from one to six leaves in the scarred dining-room table, baked a whole ham as only Mamma could, and then supplemented it with fried chicken. There were almost always several kinds of cake waiting for us, and sometimes she put the menfolk to turning the handle of the big ice cream freezer. Even so, we knew the cupboard also held freshly baked pies. No family dinner was complete for Mamma without at least two kinds of dessert.

In the wintertime there were wood-chopping chores for the men to share, for the big fireplaces consumed wood fast. Even after gas heaters were installed in most of the rooms, we loved the merry crackle and cheery warmth of the open fire.

Smoke curled from both tall chimneys, one on each side of the house, this winter night. All the family had gathered again, with the exception of Red who had died the year before. And Papa. The big house hummed with talk, but the laughter and the gaiety that had always marked such reunions were missing. For that day we had laid Papa to rest. Without any fuss or bother, he had quietly lain down and died. Did it matter that his deathbed had been the good earth he loved so much? He had been granted his oft expressed wish to wear out rather than rust out. He had been busy about his Lord's work all day, and at dusk we had found him lying in eternal sleep beside his barnyard gate. It couldn't have been more to his liking if he had carefully arranged it himself.

So there weren't any tears that winter night. Pride in him had crowded them out. In the first shock of our loss we had wept bitterly, flailing ourselves for every small hurt we had ever given him. But now we spoke in muted tones of his good life and how much he was loved in the town, the evidence of which we had seen that day.

The church in which he had begun his ministry more than thirty-five years before—a handsome brick structure now—had been crowded beyond its capacity for the simple funeral service, with many standing outside in the cold wind. Among these were twenty or thirty weeping Negroes, waiting to see their beloved friend taken on his last ride.

Inside the church, women sobbed audibly and men unashamedly wiped their eyes as the long procession filed past the flower-draped casket. Among them were the same deacons and lay leaders who had once branded Papa a traitor because he had preached the universality of God's love. Watching them that day, I had understood how fully Papa had forgiven. Like his Lord, he had loved too freely to have room in his heart for resentments. Love had triumphed, and it had been rewarded in kind. Vaguely I sensed that these men now grieving sincerely over his passing had all but forgotten they had ever treated him badly. Didn't forgiveness really demand forgetfulness?

There were so many flowers in the church. Papa hadn't looked right lying there among banks of carnations and hothouse roses, his work-roughened hands folded across his chest. Somehow they made his rugged features, untouched by marks of illness, look almost harsh by contrast. And the old blue serge suit, which Mamma had insisted he must wear, didn't go well with that blanket of lilies of the valley we had ordered. The boys had wanted to buy Papa a new suit to be buried in, but Mamma wouldn't hear to it. "It's just a waste," she said flatly. "Nobody will see the places in the seat where I've darned. If it was good enough for him to wear while he was alive, it's good enough now."

So Papa had lain in a cheap casket—again Mamma wouldn't have any other kind, saying Papa wouldn't like it—and it had hurt to see how incongruous he looked among all those delicate flowers. Then we saw an underprivileged, mentally retarded young girl stop beside the bier and smile down at him as happily as when he had often visited with her. She leaned over and dropped an odd-looking bouquet on Papa's chest before moving on.

It wasn't until the family were left alone in the church to say our last farewells that we saw the nature of the bouquet the girl had brought him. It was composed entirely of dried weeds and a dead cotton stalk with wisps of white lint clinging to the brittle bole, tied with a faded and crumpled ribbon.

None of us made a move to take it away. I think we all shared the same thought—that it seemed more appropriate for Papa than all the elaborate floral arrangements. Suddenly he looked like himself. Even the blue suit no longer mattered. And we understood also why the girl had smiled at Papa as she had. He was smiling. Why hadn't we noticed that before? Or had he been smiling before? I couldn't be sure, and I was afraid to ask.

No one mentioned Papa's special bouquet that night, though we talked of other incidents that had helped take the sting from our sorrow—of the Presbyterian banker's talk in which he said, "Brother Reaves was a true follower of Christ, too big for one church or one town and yet too humble to be aware of it"; of the old Negro who had spoken to Papa exactly as though he could hear him, "Passun Reaves, suh, I hopes you have me a seat up there real close to you"; and of the two colored men who had knocked on the kitchen door that morning to give Mamma money they said they owed the parson, but about which Mamma knew nothing at all.

Finally we sat silent, listening to the hissing of green logs on the fire and the wind moaning about the eaves of the house. Mamma stood up, her vivid blue eyes, looking even brighter in contrast to her white hair, moving from face to face as though in search of help for the ordeal of living ahead of her. Then she voiced the first complaint we had heard from her.

"I'm going to miss him." Into the short sentence was crowded all the pathos and heartbreak of ending a marriage of fifty-eight years.

None of us offered to accompany her to that lonely upstairs bedroom. We knew she would reject any such offers. This was something she had to face, and who of us had ever seen Mamma fail to stand up to a situation?

So we watched her climb the stairs, and it was as though we were watching the years glide by with each slow step she took. At the top she suddenly lifted her head and straightened her round shoulders, then moved on with her usual briskness. As the door to the bedroom closed softly I had the weird feeling that Mamma hadn't gone in alone after all.

Rusty broke the silence that held us, his eyes shining with the tears he was too proud to let us see fall. "Ennen, why don't you write a book about Papa? It ought to be a dandy."

I shook my head. "He wasn't important enough. You don't write biographies about unknown saints like Papa."

A few years ago I changed my mind. While on a visit to our national capital I went to see the tomb of the Unknown Soldier, and the imposing monument and the uniformed guard impressed me with what it meant to our American traditions to honor the humble who served as best they could without pomp or glory. Such are the very lifeblood of American history and American culture.

Papa was one of those, unknown as far as worldly fame was concerned but immortal in his far-reaching influence. By sowing the seeds of Christianity in the hearts with which he came in contact, he did his part toward defeating a spreading communistic ideology, even though he never heard the hated term. By carrying peace and love in his own heart, he contributed toward the peace of the whole world.

Yes, to the best he knew, Papa was a saint. But the trouble with saints is that they often make others feel guilty by contrast, and thus they encourage sinning. So Papa, bless his memory, may have had to answer for a lot of missteps his offspring took in spite of his own unquestionable virtues.